Presented To:

_____

By:

_____

Date:

_____

TRUTH
UNPLUGGED

**Stories for Girls on Faith, Love,
and Things That Matter Most**

HONOR  BOOKS

Inspiration and Motivation for the Season of Life

An Imprint of Cook Communications Ministries
COLORADO SPRINGS, COLORADO • PARIS, ONTARIO
KINGSWAY COMMUNICATIONS, LTD., EASTBOURNE, ENGLAND

Honor Books® is an imprint of
Cook Communications Ministries, Colorado Springs, CO 80918
Cook Communications, Paris, Ontario
Kingsway Communications, Eastbourne, England

TRUTH UNPLUGGED–
STORIES FOR GIRLS ON FAITH, LOVE, AND THINGS THAT MATTER MOST
© 2004 by BORDON BOOKS
© 2004 by COOK COMMUNICATIONS MINISTRIES

First printing, 2004
Printed in the UNITED STATES OF AMERICA
2 3 4 5 6 Printing/Year 08 07 06 05 04

Developed by Bordon Books
6532 E. 71st Street, Suite 105
Tulsa, OK 74133

Manuscript written by Gena Maselli.

Scripture quotations marked NIV are taken from the *Holy Bible, New International Version®*. NIV®. Copyright © 1973, 1978, 1984 by International Bible Society. Used by permission of Zondervan Publishing House. All rights reserved. Scripture quotations marked NKJV are taken from *The New King James Version*. Copyright © 1979, 1980, 1982, Thomas Nelson, Inc; NASB are taken from the *New American Standard Bible*. Copyright © The Lockman Foundation 1960, 1962, 1963, 1968, 1971, 1972, 1973, 1975, 1977, 1995. Used by permission; THE MESSAGE are taken from *The Message*, copyright © by Eugene H. Peterson, 1993, 1994, 1995, 1996. Used by permission of NavPress Publishing Group.

ISBN 1-56292-207-6

INTRODUCTION

Life is serious. And life as a teen is something God takes very seriously. Often it is difficult to separate yourself from the world and its way of doing things. But God wants you set apart for Him, unplugged from the deception of the world so that you can see God's better plan—*Truth Unplugged.*

What? You don't believe it?

Put David as a teen in front of Goliath, hurling stones with the force of a bullet to break a stalemate no adult in his time could manage. Or how about this? Send the Son of God to earth as a helpless baby and make Him the sole, 24/7 responsibility of a fourteen to sixteen-year-old mother named Mary. Or call a shy, sensitive teen named Jeremiah and tell him to be the bearer of bad news to a king and his court, adults whose lives are way out of control. Oh, and tell him they will hate him and will never listen to him.

See what God means? He takes *you* just as seriously.

Youth for God is just another name for serious, out-of-the-box adventurers. That's why we've collected these stories about teens dealing with some pretty heavy stuff. Because you are dealing with important, life-altering issues every day—stuff sometimes your parents know nothing about. The decisions you make are often made under pressures that would make any adult cave in no time—but you can't cave. You have your future ahead of you, and you plan to make it a good one. That's why it's so important to have God's reality—His *Truth Unplugged* for your life.

So here are some stories about decisive moments in people's lives that look a lot like yours. And at the end of each story is a verse from the Bible, just so you know what God has to say about these issues—a **Download** of what He has to say to you. And there is a **Truth Link**—prayer where you can tell God what you need and ask for His help. In **Power Up** you will find questions or challenges that hold you accountable for your decisions and bring you face-to-face with implications that aren't always obvious. Sometimes you might feel like **Power Up** is in your face, but it will bring the truth to you from a very honest perspective and hopefully give you a true reflection of your heart. Finally, there is **Truth Unplugged**—a rule of thumb to help you remember what to do when life is moving a little fast, and someone is tapping their foot, pushing you to go their way. It can help you go God's way. Because, like we said—okay, you get the picture—your life is serious business, so serious that sometimes you are the only one God can count on to do the right thing.

Don't let anyone put you down because you're young.
1 Timothy 4:12 THE MESSAGE

TABLE OF CONTENTS

Introduction 5

The Life Filter (Dating) 9

No Man's Land (Divorce) 14

The Chilling Truth (Anger) 19

Whom to Trust? (Pregnancy).........................25

Family Keys (Family Changes).......................31

What's the Big Deal? (Drugs) 37

Nothing but the Truth (Gossip) 43

Fuzzy Memories (Drinking) 49

The Courage to Run (Courage) 55

Not My Problem (Eating Disorders) 60

Stick with It (Diligence) 66

A Missed Friendship (Cliques) 71

Her Brother's Secret (Joy) 77

Second-String Plan (Pride)...........................82

Reflection (Materialism) 87

The Challenge (Mentoring)............................92

A Cross in the Road (Stealing/Shoplifting)...........97

Not the End of the World (Peace)....................102

Face the Truth (Forgiveness)........................108

The Best Birthday Present Ever (Love)...............113

First Impressions (Judging Others) 118

The Double Life (Church) 123

Defending Her Territory (Jealousy).................128

Scars (Inner Healing from Abuse) 133

Someone Who Understands (Loneliness)..............137

The Proof of Life (Prayer)............................141

The Sacrifice (Giving)..................................145

The Prom Night Decision (Sex) 150

Turn on the Light (Encouragement) 156

The Grace to Live at Home (Difficult Parents) 161

Shattered into a Million Pieces (Heartbreak) 166

Making the Time Count (Attitude) 172

Aftermath (Fear) 177

It's Not a Date! (Manipulation) 181

Anything I Want (Lying) 186

Big Bird, Chubby, and Other Frizz (Image) 192

Get Outta My Life! (Sibling Rivalry) 197

We're in This Together (Illness) 202

Getting the Whole Story (Criticism) 207

Got It Pretty Good (Thankfulness) 212

Worth More Than That (Modesty) 217

Unlovable (Suicide) 223

Common Ground (Friendship) 228

The Driving Dilemma (Patience) 233

More Beautiful Than You Can Imagine (Death) 238

What about Them? (Racism) 243

A World of Difference (Salvation) 248

TOPICAL INDEX 255

THE LIFE FILTER

Dating

⟨♨⟩ **DOWNLOAD:**

You are A CHOSEN RACE, A ROYAL PRIESTHOOD, A HOLY NATION, A PEOPLE FOR GOD'S OWN POSSESSION, so that you may proclaim the excellencies of Him who has called you out of darkness into His marvelous light. 1 Peter 2:9 NASB

"Hey, Trish, thank God I found you! Guess what I just heard?" Liz exclaimed, racing up to Trish in the hall between classes. "You'll never guess!"

Trish stood at her open locker, grabbing her biology notebook before slamming the door. "What?"

"Hunter Stevens is going to ask you out! Can you believe it? The hottest guy in school! I overheard him talking to Brett Coleson in the lunch line. He said you sit near him in biology. He thinks you're pretty and smart. According to him, you've got the 'whole package.' Can you believe it?" Liz paused to take a much-needed breath before continuing, "Why aren't you jumping up and down? Here I am ready to do a toe-touch for you."

"Liz, of course I'm flattered," Trish said, choosing her words all too carefully. "Actually I'm stunned. And you're right; he is the hottest guy in school."

"But?"

"But isn't he a little wild? I mean, weren't he and the rest of the football team busted for drinking at the last away game? They even sneaked it onto the bus. How stupid is that?"

"Trish, we're talking about Hunter Stevens. *The* Hunter Stevens. The guy we've dreamed about since junior high. Come on. Don't tell me you'd let one screw-up keep you from dating him!"

Liz couldn't believe what she was hearing. Trish was actually debating whether she would go out with Hunter Stevens. Dating him would make her a part of the most popular crowd in school. As a cheerleader, Liz hung out with most of the kids in the group anyway, but even she wasn't up there with Hunter Stevens. *How in the world could Trish consider turning him down?* she wondered.

She and Trish had been friends since elementary school. In fact, Trish had been her first friend. They grew up just a few blocks away from each other and even attended the same church. But sometimes Trish could be a stickler about her faith. Liz prided herself on her own open-mindedness. *We basically believe the same way,* Liz reasoned. She tried to understand Trish's convictions, but sometimes she thought Trish just needed to lighten up.

Liz had no problem dating someone who didn't believe the way she did. In her mind, life had compartments. School was school, church was church, and guys were—well, guys. Liz didn't see why all the areas had to overlap.

Trish, on the other hand, believed that church extended into every area of her life. She once told Liz that she viewed her life like a filter. Hobbies, guys, friends, and school—everything went through the filter. If it didn't line up with her faith, then she set it aside. To Liz, that kind of reasoning made life *way* too difficult. There was plenty of time for that serious stuff later.

Liz could barely concentrate the rest of the day. Maybe if Trish went out with Hunter, she would finally get a chance with Brett Coleson. Not only was he a hottie, but he also had a sweet car. She had tried to get his attention over the last few months. She went to the same parties—sometimes alone, since Trish wouldn't go with her, and her other friends had boyfriends.

When she had told Trish about her plans to snag Brett, Trish had questioned her, "Is he a Christian?" As if being a Christian was some sort of litmus test.

"I don't know. I guess. I'm sure he believes in God. He's probably just like us," she replied.

But now, this was their chance. Trish could get together with Hunter, and Liz could go out with Brett. It sounded like an excellent plan to her. If they were lucky, they could make it

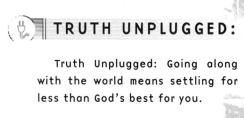

TRUTH UNPLUGGED:

Truth Unplugged: Going along with the world means settling for less than God's best for you.

through the year with the hottest boyfriends in school.

After school, Liz raced back to Trish's locker, eager to hear the news. "Well?" she asked when Trish finally arrived.

"Well, what?" Trish said, opening her locker and unloading her backpack.

"So? Did he ask you? What'd he say?"

"He asked me to go out with him and some of his friends on Friday."

"Oh, man, that is so cool! You are so in with his crowd!"

Pausing from unpacking, Trish confessed, "I turned him down."

"You what?" Liz was positive she misheard.

"I turned him down. He's not a Christian, and I can't go out with him. You know I don't date guys who aren't Christians."

"You're kidding, right?" Liz asked, her eyes wide with disbelief. "I know you said you wouldn't, but I didn't really think you could turn Hunter Stevens down," she said slowly, as if trying to absorb the shock.

"It wasn't easy, but . . . it was the right thing to do."

Liz continued to watch her friend and then finally said, "Okay, if that's what you want, I'm okay with that."

"Liz, I know you don't understand, but honestly, I don't understand you either," Trish said gently. "How can you go to church on Sundays and Wednesdays and then go to wild parties and date non-Christians. You have other choices, you know?"

Trish's words stung. Liz knew there was truth in them, but why couldn't she have it all—church *and* popular boyfriends? Or did she really have to choose? "Why is it so wrong to do both? It's not like I'm going to marry these guys. I just want to have fun. And they're popular and good-looking. What's so wrong with that?" Liz questioned.

"There's nothing wrong with being popular or good-looking, but you know you have nothing in common with them—at least not anything that really matters."

Liz shrugged. "Maybe." Perhaps Trish was right. Maybe she couldn't separate the areas of her life as much as she pretended she could. Maybe she should make more of a distinction. She had to think about it.

"Are you coming to youth group tomorrow night?" Trish asked, trying to lighten the moment.

"Huh? Oh, yeah, sure," Liz answered, her mind a thousand miles away.

TRUTH LINK:

Dear Lord, thank You for showing me the best way to live and the right people to have in my life. Help me to be strong so that I will live my life the way You want me to live, making good choices in all my relationships. Help me to choose the right friends and dates. In fact, let them be the ones You handpick for me. Amen.

POWER UP:

Have you ever been swayed into thinking or acting a certain way by the people around you? Friends and family won't always understand your convictions, but don't fall into the trap of just going with the flow. It may seem like a sacrifice in the short run, but remember, God desires that you have relationships with people who share your faith—not because He's punishing you, but because He knows what's best for you.

NO MAN'S LAND

Divorce

> I know the plans I have for you . . . plans to prosper you and not to harm you, plans to give you hope and a future.
>
> Jeremiah 29:11 NIV

"So, when is your dad coming to pick you up?" Michelle's mother asked, standing in her bedroom doorway.

"He said he'd be here around 6:30," Michelle responded, packing her bag for a weekend with her father.

"Is *she* going to be there?"

"Who?"

"Little Miss Aerobics Instructor," her mother sneered.

"I don't know, Mom," Michelle said with resignation. *When will this ever end?* she wondered sadly.

"Well, she's so young, she probably still has a curfew. So even if she is there, she probably won't be able to stay long."

Michelle's parents had divorced the previous year. It hadn't come as a surprise since their home had been a war zone for years, full of screaming matches followed by frosty silences. Michelle preferred the screaming. At least then she had understood her place in the mix. The silent conflicts, however, had crept into every corner of the house, making it impossible for her to relax.

After her parents' divorce, Michelle thought it would get better. At least, if they weren't living together, there would be peace, she'd reasoned.

That had been an illusion.

Michelle now lived in "no man's land" between the two rival camps. She spent every other weekend and one or two dinners a week with her dad. The rest of the time she lived with her mom.

Her parents didn't talk to each other anymore. Instead, they talked *through* Michelle or their lawyers. Through her, they tried to find out as much as possible about the other. Who each dated? How much money the other had. What kind of car he or she drove now. Their jobs. Anything and everything. They congratulated themselves when they discovered that the other one was having difficulties. Michelle's mom was convinced that her dad was in the midst of a mid-life crisis, and her dad was equally certain her mother had become a nagging shrew who didn't know how to have a good time.

Michelle didn't see either of them that way. They just approached life differently. Her levelheaded mother preferred simplicity and frugality. Her generous father, always the life of the party, thrived on spontaneity. Michelle loved them both but found it difficult to always be in the middle.

She tried not to dwell on whether they had any regrets about having her. *Maybe if they'd never had me, they'd be happier,* she thought. *They'd be able to get on with their lives without having to see each other again. But because of me, they are stuck with a connection to each other forever.*

Michelle shook her head, trying to escape that harassing thought. She continued stuffing clothes and makeup into her bag. Her mom hadn't stopped complaining about her father or his younger girlfriend.

"I just can't believe he's not embarrassed to date her. She's half his age," she said. Then she mumbled, "But what do I know? I lived with him for 17 years and I still don't understand him."

Abruptly, a truck horn honked. Michelle's mom walked to the window. "He's here."

"I'm ready."

"Do you have your jacket?" she asked. "It could get chilly this weekend. Oh, and by the way, I'll be over at Grandma's tomorrow, so if you need me, call me on my cell phone. I love you," she said, giving her daughter a hug. "Have fun."

"I love you too, Mom. I'll see you on Sunday." Michelle grabbed her jacket and her purse and walked out the door.

"Hey, sweetheart," her dad called, opening the truck door from the inside. "Guess what we're going to do?"

Too excited to wait for a reply, he continued. "We're going waterskiing! I have a friend at work who invited us out to his place for the weekend. He lives on Lake Kipaushee. His daughter is visiting him too, and he has a motorboat so we can waterski. And we're gonna have a cookout. It'll be a blast! Come on; get in. We can head out there now."

"That sounds like fun, Dad." Her weekends with her dad were *never* boring.

As they drove away, Michelle's dad asked her about friends and school. Then the conversation turned to her mother. "How's your mom?"

Here it comes, Michelle thought. "She's fine."

"She got big plans this weekend?" he smirked, shaking his head. "Don't answer that. As if your mother ever has big plans. She'll probably sit at home alone and read a book."

Michelle turned and stared out the window.

"Hey, I'm just playing around," her dad said.

"No, you're not," Michelle said quietly under her breath.

"What was that?"

Turning to face her father, she spoke evenly. "You're not joking, Dad. You and Mom never joke about each other. You just trash each other. You used to trash each other face-to-face. Now, you just trash each other to me."

Michelle's dad stared straight ahead.

"You guys probably wish I'd never been born so you could be rid of each other," Michelle murmured, turning back toward the window.

TRUTH UNPLUGGED:

Although things in your life may be difficult now, God's picture of your future is full of great things.

Michelle's dad shot her a surprised look. "What'd you just say?"

"I said you probably wish I'd never been born so you could be rid of each other once and for all."

Her dad pulled his truck over to the side of the road, allowing other cars to pass. He turned to her and said, "Sweetheart, I want you to hear me on this. Your mother and I have never wished you hadn't been born. I know things have been tough, but there's one thing we agree on and that's you. You are the best thing that ever happened to either of us. And I'm sorry our bickering has made you think you are anything but a gift to us."

Michelle didn't say anything. She stared down at her hands, trying to hold back the tears in her eyes.

"I'll tell you what," her dad continued in a gentle voice. "I'll call your mom. I'm not promising that we'll be perfect, but I'll talk to her about how we can work together to keep you out of our problems."

Then, pulling Michelle into a hug, he choked, "I love you. Don't ever doubt that you're the best thing in my life."

TRUTH LINK:

Dear Lord, please help me to live in peace in my home. Show me how to be an example to my family and how to approach each day the way You want me to live. I know that You love me. Help me to remember that You have plans for my life and not to entertain thoughts that life would be better without me. Amen.

POWER UP:

Have you ever lived in the aftermath of an ugly divorce? Maybe your parents' divorce was somewhat friendly. If so, great. Unfortunately, many times that's not the case. With some divorced parents, the battle continues to rage, leaving kids feeling caught in the middle. If that's you, ask God to show you how to live and respond to their anger in love and peace. Allow Him to show you how to be an example and refuse to give in to thoughts that their problems are your fault, or that life would be better off without you. Your life was planned from the beginning, and God still has good plans for you and your future.

THE CHILLING TRUTH

Anger

> DOWNLOAD:

Be quick to listen, slow to speak and slow to become angry, for man's anger does not bring about the righteous life that God desires. James 1:19-20 NIV

"How could they do this to me?" Erica seethed. Her parents had promised one of her father's new co-workers that her son could hang out with Erica at the carnival on Saturday night.

"Be nice, Erica," her father had said. "He's new in town and doesn't know anyone. You can take him to the carnival and introduce him to your friends. It'll be fun." Erica rolled her eyes just remembering the conversation. Her parents were always interfering in her life. They couldn't force her to be friends with some loser. Whether he was new in town or not wasn't her problem.

On Saturday, her father drove her over to pick up J.T., his coworker's son, to take them to the carnival. Erica took one look at J.T. and rolled her eyes again. As he crawled in the backseat of the car, she gave him her best we're-not-going-to-be-friends stare. As far as she was concerned, he could look like Brad Pitt, be as smart as Bill Gates, and as funny as Jim Carrey, they *still* wouldn't be friends. Her parents had forced her into this, and unfortunately for him, *he* was going to pay for it.

On the way to the carnival, Erica's dad tried to make small talk with J.T. He even went as far as to try to draw Erica into the conversation too, but she wouldn't have it. She gave him one-word answers in a clipped tone. She wasn't going to play into his I'm-such-a-cool-Dad persona. J.T. answered her dad's questions and even asked some of his own in return.

Well, aren't they hitting it off? Erica thought sarcastically. *Maybe Dad should take him to the carnival so I can have fun with my friends instead of baby-sitting some loser.*

At the carnival, Erica jumped out of the car and slammed the door. She was ready to leave J.T. in the dust when she heard her father call to her through the driver's window. Stopping with a halt, she turned and walked to the car. "What is your problem, Erica? You can be angry at your mom and me, but don't take it out on J.T. He didn't do anything."

Erica responded with a cold, "Fine," before turning back toward J.T.

Passing him on the way to the ticket counter, she threw out a tense, "Come on." Not waiting for him to respond, she went to buy tickets.

Afterwards, Erica saw a group of her friends sitting near the concession stands. She made a beeline for the group, leaving J.T. to follow at a distance. When he arrived, Erica watched as several of her friends introduced themselves to J.T. and invited him to join them. Erica, on the other hand, ignored him at every turn.

"Where'd you meet J.T.?" her friend Cybil asked when he'd gone to buy nachos.

"My parents," she said with disdain. "His mother works with my father. He's new in town, and my dad offered to have him come to the carnival with me. Can you believe it?"

Cybil laughed and shook her head. "I don't know what you're so angry about. He's cool."

Erica rolled her eyes again. "Please," she responded, as though Cybil had said the most ridiculous thing in the world.

As everyone ate all the nachos, hot dogs, and cotton candy they could stand, Erica noticed how much her friends seemed to like J.T. They included him in all the jokes and conversations. Because she was still irritated, she couldn't bring herself to join in the fun. He was an outsider who had finagled his way into her group of friends. They may not care how he had come to join their group, but she did. She wasn't going to act like everything was okay because it wasn't.

In the middle of one of J.T.'s jokes, Erica suddenly stood up, interrupting him. "Are we gonna ride some rides, or are we just going to sit here wasting time?" Then she walked to a trash can and threw her nacho tray away. She knew she'd been rude by the startled look on J.T.'s face when she interrupted him. In fact, everyone had looked surprised by her outburst, but she couldn't help herself. These were her friends, not his.

As the group made their way to the Tilt-A-Wheel, they decided who would ride with whom. Erica wasn't thrilled about riding with J.T., but it didn't look like she had much of a choice. The others had decided for her. J.T., Cybil, and Erica were in one car. After handing her ticket to the ticket taker at the front of the line, she made her way over to an available car. "Miss, please step this way," one of the workers called, summoning her to a different car. "That one is out of order."

Erica scowled and entered the car indicated by the worker. "Did you hear how he spoke to me?" she hissed to Cybil after they'd all sat down. "He doesn't have to give me that attitude.

How was I supposed to know that car was out of order?" Cybil only chuckled, while J.T. looked blankly at Erica.

After the Tilt-A-Wheel, they made their way to a few other rides before heading to the Ferris wheel. Again, Erica was paired with J.T. Though they sat next to each other in the chair, neither of them spoke. Inching their way to the top, the Ferris wheel stopped at intervals, allowing other passengers to get on and off. Once at the top, Erica could see for miles. She wasn't especially fond of heights and grew anxious with each passing moment. "What is the problem? Why can't they get this thing going?" she said in frustration, looking anxiously over the edge.

"Are you *always* so angry?" J.T. asked. Erica turned to find him watching her with a questioning look in his eyes.

"What's that supposed to mean?" she responded hotly.

"You've been angry since I met you. At first I thought you were just angry with your dad. Then I thought it must be me. Now you've smarted off twice about the carnival workers. You're just looking for a fight, aren't you?"

Erica felt the sting of his words, but she couldn't bring herself to admit he was right. "What do you know?" she answered in disgust. "My parents make me drag along some guy I don't even know to this stupid carnival. Then you try to act like you're a part of my group of friends when you're not. Now, I have to put up with stupid people who can't even run a Tilt-A-Wheel or a Ferris wheel. I mean, what kind of brains do you need to push the button?"

At the end of her tirade, she expected J.T. to respond. In fact, she welcomed it. *Bring it on!* she thought. Instead, J.T. simply watched her. After several silent moments, Erica began to feel uneasy, but J.T. didn't flinch. He just continued to look at her as though she were a puzzle to be solved. Then slowly he smiled before simply adding, "Well, I guess I rest my case." Erica felt stunned. She'd expected a fight, and instead he was laughing at her. She wanted to knock him out of the seat.

After the ride, the group went to play a few games. They threw pennies into fishbowls, knocked down bowling pins with base-balls, and tossed rings around soda bottles. Several of the others had won trinkets and stuffed animals for their efforts, but Erica couldn't seem to win anything. The harder she tried, the angrier she got. Finally, after playing several games, she was on the verge of giving up. "Stupid game!" she shouted, hitting the counter with her fist.

"Just relax," J.T. said, coming up beside her. "You're letting your emotions throw off your game. Take a few deep breaths and try it like this." Effortlessly, he threw the basketball into the hole. "Come on; you try." Erica waited to hear sarcasm from him. Instead, he seemed to genuinely care that she win a prize. Taking his advice, she took deep breaths and aimed for the hole.

Swoosh. In it went.

Then she tried another. *Swoosh*.

And another. *Swoosh*.

With her Tweety Bird tucked securely under her arm, she turned to J.T. "Thanks," she said simply. He nodded, smiled, and walked to the next game.

Watching him go, Erica thought back to his question

TRUTH UNPLUGGED:

You don't have to feel like a volcano that's ready to explode when difficult situations come up. God can help free you from a bad temper.

earlier. Was she really angry all the time? Was she always looking for a fight? She had to admit that she was. She usually felt like a pressure cooker ready to explode, which explained why she was usually at odds with her parents and so protective of her friend-ships. She expected the worst from people, so she was always on the defensive.

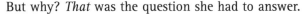

But why? *That* was the question she had to answer.

Looking up at the stars and the moon in the night sky, she realized that God was the only One who could help her answer that question. And He was definitely the only One who could help her change. *Lord, I don't know why I get angry so quickly,* she prayed silently, *but it's how I feel most of the time. I don't want to push people away and always expect the worst from them. I want to be at peace and take things as they come—calmly. You can help me with that, can't You?*

Feeling the night breeze stir, Erica hugged her Tweety a little closer and ran to rejoin her friends, knowing that together, she and God were going to work on it.

TRUTH LINK:

Dear Lord, I struggle with anger. Little things set me off. I try to control my temper, but sometimes it still gets the best of me. Please help me to respond with compassion and self-control when dealing with other people and things. And when I do get angry, help me to walk away from the situation rather than act on it. Amen.

POWER UP:

Do you have a temper? Do you become so angry sometimes that you just want to throw something or hurt someone? Are you always on the defensive because you expect the worst from people? God can help. He can help you develop more patience, show you what triggers your anger, and teach you how to deal with it. For instance, He might show you how to communicate your feelings in a respectful, clear manner. Or He may help you think the best of others instead of automatically feeling defensive. He can help you stay calm in the midst of irritating situations.

WHOM TO TRUST?

Pregnancy

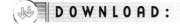

DOWNLOAD:

You are my refuge in the day of disaster.

Jeremiah 17:17 NASB

O God, please, no. Brittany silently pleaded, placing the home pregnancy test on the sink.

If this turns out positive, I don't know what I'll do, she thought. *My parents will kill me. Jason will freak. This can't be happening. I'm only sixteen.*

Just then, she glanced down and saw two pink stripes. Grabbing the box she compared the results. One stripe, not pregnant. Two stripes, pregnant.

She froze, unable to breathe.

Her head spun. *This can't be real.* The words flashed over and over in her mind.

Knock, knock, knock.

"Brittany, are you ready? Julie's here. You're gonna be late for school if you don't hurry," her mother called through the door.

She grabbed her backpack, stuffed the test inside, and opened the door to see her mother's concerned face.

"Are you okay?" her mother asked. "You don't look like you feel very well," she said, placing the back of her hand to Brittany's forehead. She searched Brittany's face.

"I'm fine, Mom. I'm just tired. I think I stayed up too late studying," Brittany said, avoiding her mother's eyes.

Walking through the kitchen, Brittany passed on the toast her mother had prepared for breakfast. The sight of it made her stomach roll.

"Aren't you going to have breakfast?" her mother asked, knowing Brittany never skipped breakfast.

"No, I'll grab something at school," Brittany mumbled, walking out the garage door. She'd have cried if it weren't for the fact that her mother would get her to confess to what was wrong. She couldn't face her mom yet . . . and she couldn't even imagine facing her dad.

Climbing into Julie's car, music blared. Julie checked her makeup and moved to the beat of the music. Seeing Brittany, she called out, "What's wrong with you? You look like somebody died."

"I'm fine," Brittany responded. Julie was one of her closest friends, but she wouldn't understand. In fact, Brittany wasn't sure *whom* she could tell. Though her friends were fun to hang out with, the news of her pregnancy would spread, and the last thing Brittany wanted was for this to get out.

O God, this can't be happening to me, she thought desperately, staring out the window as they made their way to school.

Throughout the day, it was hard for Brittany to concentrate on anything. Everything was a blur. Her friends tried to talk to her at lunch, but she barely heard anything they said. *What am I going to do?* she asked herself as she picked at her salad. She couldn't eat. The despair and fear she felt left little room for anything else in her stomach.

Across the cafeteria, she saw Jason laughing with his friends, not a care in the world. *How would he respond?* she wondered. They had started dating five months ago, around Thanksgiving. Brittany had liked him for a while, so when he asked her to go to the Thanksgiving Day parade, she had been ecstatic. He was good-looking, smart, and fun to hang out with.

Their relationship had been intense from the beginning. They hadn't planned for things to go as far as they had. They had let their emotions and feelings take over. It was like a fire she couldn't put out—until it was too late. It had been the first time for both of them. At the time, she'd thought it was so romantic, like something out of a movie. Now, watching him across the cafeteria, she realized they never should have gone as far as they had. They simply weren't prepared for what might happen.

Pregnancy happens to other girls, Brittany had always told herself. It happened to trashy girls who slept around, not sixteen-year-old honor-roll students who planned to go to college, went to church on Sunday, and had two parents who were involved in their lives. Feeling like she needed fresh air, Brittany left the cafeteria.

She dragged herself through the rest of her classes. At the end of the day, Jason waited by her locker. "Hey, what's up?" he asked, leaning down to give her a kiss. "You still want to go to Joe's party on Saturday night. It'll be a blast. His parents are outta town, ya know?" He raised his eyebrows up and down.

"Um, I don't think I can," Brittany said.

"Why not? You wanted to go last week."

"Something's come up," Brittany said quietly.

"What?" he asked, an invisible question mark on his face.

"Jason, we need to talk, but not here. Drive me home, and I'll tell you in the car."

Before leaving the school parking lot, Brittany told Jason the truth and showed him the pregnancy test. As she spoke, he stared at it, not saying a word.

Then quietly he asked, "What are you gonna do?"

"What do you mean, what am I going to do?" she asked incredulously.

"You know what I mean, Brittany." He sounded defeated. "I can't handle this. I'm only sixteen. I can't have a kid or be a father."

Stunned, Brittany suddenly knew the truth—the truth that had been gnawing at her all day. She was alone. Tears that she'd held at bay rose to her eyes. *O God, please help me,* she prayed.

The drive home was tense. Brittany just wanted to get out of the car. This was the end for her and Jason. She thought she would be more upset about their breakup, but in the light of the pregnancy, their relationship seemed weak.

"You haven't told anybody at school, have you?" Jason asked when they'd arrived at her house.

"No."

"Good, I wouldn't want this getting around." He sounded relieved.

"Jason, I'm pregnant," she threw out, wondering what alternate universe he thought they lived in. "I can't hide this forever."

"You could always have an abortion," he offered.

"Shut up, Jason!" she yelled. He wasn't offering a solution for her. He was trying to save his own skin. "*I'll* decide what *I'm* going to do. *You* can't handle this, remember?" With that, she jumped out of the car, slamming the door.

Opening the front door, Brittany smelled the banana bread her mother was baking. It was Brittany's favorite.

"Hey, honey," her mother called from the kitchen. "Since you were so tired this morning and have been working so hard, I thought we'd have your favorites for dinner—chicken and dumplings with banana bread for dessert."

Brittany stopped at the kitchen entrance, watching her mother. Suddenly, she broke, tears flowing down her cheeks.

Her mother rushed to her side. "Brittany, what's wrong?"

Brittany couldn't speak. She could only sob. She cried so hard that her legs buckled.

Her mother caught her. "Honey, what's wrong? Come here and sit down," she said, leading Brittany to a chair. She knelt in front of her daughter, desperately trying to understand Brittany's breakdown. "Honey, tell me. Tell me everything. We'll fix it. I promise."

Brittany looked up at her mother. "Mom, I'm pregnant," she whispered, waiting for her mother's anger and condemnation. Instead, looking into her mother's eyes, she saw shock followed by tears.

Without saying a word, her mother wrapped her arms around her, and together they wept. Moments later her mother composed herself. "I don't know what to say, Brittany, except that with God's help, we'll manage. Let's pray about this and we'll talk to your father as soon as he gets home."

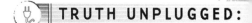

TRUTH UNPLUGGED:

You can trust God with anything in your life—any decision, mistake, or success. Open your heart and tell Him everything. He really wants to know.

Relieved at her mother's reaction, Brittany nodded and forced a smile through her tears.

TRUTH LINK:

Dear Lord, You know everything—my actions, my thoughts, my fears, and my hopes—even before I do. So You already know I've made a mistake. I ask for Your forgiveness and Your help. I don't know what to do. I don't know who else to trust but You. Show me what I should do and to whom I should talk. Amen.

POWER UP:

Are you in a situation and you don't know the answers to the questions swirling about in your mind? Have you made a mistake, and you fear that the people around you and God will never forgive you? The good news is that God will always forgive you. He already knows everything you've done—good and bad. He doesn't want to punish you. He wants to help. Let Him be a refuge, a place of safety for you. Let Him be the One you go to with everything in your life. People are willing and able to help you. Ask for God's guidance.

FAMILY KEYS

Family Changes

DOWNLOAD:

Let petitions and praises shape your worries into prayers,
letting God know your concerns. Before you know it, a sense of
God's wholeness, everything coming together for good, will come
and settle you down. Philippians 4:6-7 THE MESSAGE

Jessica looked at the view from the top of the lighthouse. The gray ocean stretched forward as far as the eye could see, meeting the heavy, gray sky in the distance. The sea tossed and rolled. Whitecaps raced one after another toward the rocky shore.

This was the most interesting thing she'd seen on this trip. Jessica hadn't wanted to come on this trip with her father, new stepmother, and new stepsister. She would rather have been at home with her friends and boyfriend, enjoying a hot summer of swimming and working on her tan. Instead, she was forced to join these strange people her father had invited into their lives.

"The Cape Hatteras Lighthouse is the tallest lighthouse in the United States, standing 208 feet tall," the rugged-faced guide explained. "Its purpose was to help ships navigate the treacherous waters of the Diamond Shoals off our North Carolina coast."

Jessica looked over at her father, who watched the guide with intensity. That's the way her dad faced every situation—with intensity. Even this vacation was intense. Her dad had married Marie three months ago. And with Marie came Samantha, her new ten-year-old stepsister. Jessica's dad had decided that they all needed a vacation to bond as a family.

Jessica pouted. The last thing she wanted was to "bond" with these strangers. She turned to stare out at the water again. *Why did he have to get married?* she wondered again. *We were just fine without them.*

"Hey, Jessica, you ready to go? Marie and Samantha want to go to the gift shop," her dad said, coming up beside her.

"Sure, Dad," Jessica said hopelessly.

"Hey, what's this about? Aren't you having a good time?" her dad asked enthusiastically, throwing an arm around her shoulders.

"Yeah, the lighthouse is great," Jessica said with a forced smile.

"Good. Once we leave here, we're heading into town to a historical bed-and-breakfast Marie and Samantha found. Then we will find a restaurant with local cuisine. Doesn't that sound like fun?"

Jessica didn't answer. Instead, she went down the stairs wishing that they could stay in the kinds of places she and her dad usually stayed in—nice hotels. For dinner, they would have gone to a chain restaurant—one she recognized—or to a mall to shop and eat in the food court. Instead, she faced a night of weird food and frilly rooms with no TV.

Ugh! Could this trip get any worse? she wondered.

Down in the gift shop, Marie and Samantha announced they'd found the perfect souvenir for the trip—matching T-shirts. Completely thrilled with their find, they each held up T-shirts with a big picture of the black-and-white, candy-cane-painted lighthouse on the front. They were on sale, four for $35.

"We can all match!" Samantha squealed.

"Um . . . I don't think so," Jessica said, trying hard not to sound completely horrified at the thought of wearing the T-shirt, let alone matching with everyone.

"What do you mean?" Samantha asked incredulously.

"Sorry, Samantha. I'm not wearing a matching T-shirt," Jessica said rudely.

"I wouldn't want to match you anyway." Samantha shot back. "You're so snotty!" And with that, she threw the T-shirt down and ran out of the store.

Marie frowned at Jessica and then at Jessica's dad. Then, without saying a word, she placed the T-shirts back on the display and headed out to comfort Samantha.

Irritated, Jessica wasn't sure how to respond. "What's with her? All I said was that I didn't want one of these stupid T-shirts. She doesn't have to get tragic on me," Jessica said defensively.

Her dad exhaled slowly. "Jessica, Marie and I getting married is an adjustment for everyone, not just you. You're getting used to a new stepmom and stepsister. I'm getting used to a new wife and daughter. Marie's getting used to us and so is Samantha. You know, Marie told me that Samantha has always wanted a big sister. So you're an answer to a prayer for her. Instead of trying to get to know her, you brush her aside every chance you get."

Jessica felt defeated. She hadn't thought of it from anyone else's perspective. She knew only that things were difficult for her. "I just miss the way things used to be," she mumbled.

"Actually, I think things were better in your mind than they were in reality. Do you realize that since Marie and I got married, we've eaten almost every dinner together at the dining room table? I know more about what's happening with you now than I ever did before. And Marie goes out of her way to make sure you have the right clothes for school and dances. She reminds me about all your softball games and school activities so that I can be there. And on top of that, she and Samantha haven't missed one of your games either. You've gone from having zero or one person in the stands to having three people at every game rooting their hearts out for you. Trust me; you have more now than you did before. You just won't let yourself admit it."

Jessica considered what her dad had said. Maybe she hadn't realized that things were better now than they were before Marie and Samantha came into their lives. Really, she hadn't even noticed all the things they did for her. Or how much nicer things were with them there. She was too busy shutting down anytime they were around or being irritated that she had to share her dad's attention.

"Dad, can't it be just you and me sometimes?" Jessica asked hopefully. "We don't have to do *everything* as a group, do we?"

Her dad seemed to consider her question before answering. "Sure, we can do some things together—just you and me. What if we set aside some time for us to go out a few times a month? Maybe lunch, or dinner, a movie together, or something like that?"

Jessica smiled. "That'd be great, Dad." She felt the tension and fear of losing her father melt away. Finally, they would be able to have a slice of life that would be just for the two of them in the midst of getting to know her new family.

After her dad left the shop, Jessica decided to make an effort with her new family. Maybe things weren't so bad after all. Then she got an idea of how to make things up to Samantha. Glancing around the store she found exactly what she was searching for.

Back at the car, Jessica crawled into the backseat. Refusing to look at her, Samantha stared out the window, her face streaked with dried tears.

"Hey, Samantha, I found something for you," she said.

Her father and Marie turned around to listen.

"Actually," she continued, "I found something for everyone."

Samantha cautiously turned toward her. "What?"

"Well, it's not a T-shirt, but I still think it's cool." Then, out of a bag, Jessica pulled four bronze-colored key chains, which were in the shape of the lighthouse. "They're key chains from Cape Hatteras Lighthouse. We can put our house keys on them. See, we could only wear a T-shirt once in a while, but we can use these key chains every day. And we'll be the only ones with a key chain and a key to *our* house on it."

Samantha reached out and gently took her key chain, examining it carefully. "It's just for us?" she asked.

"Yeah, just for our family," Jessica said, smiling down at her. "I can't have my little sister losing her keys and getting locked out of the house, can I?"

TRUTH UNPLUGGED:

God wants to show you His perspective. He can give you hope through changes in your family.

Samantha smiled and giggled as she grasped her new lighthouse key chain.

Watching the joy on Samantha's face made Jessica realize how much fun being a big sister could turn out to be.

TRUTH LINK:

Dear Lord, my family has recently changed. I don't understand why it had to change, but I ask You to give me peace and wisdom during the transition. Help me to be patient with my new family members and let me see the good things about them. Help me to love them the way You love them. Amen.

POWER UP:

Families can be difficult to understand, and it is especially hard when stepparents, stepbrothers, and stepsisters enter your family picture. It's easy to resent the changes that they bring to your life. Things used to be one way, and now they're another. Remember that it's a change for everyone—your parent, your new stepparent, your siblings, and your new stepsiblings. It's important for everyone to find the best way to live together. Talk to your parents about your concerns and then really listen to what they have to say. Try to be patient, and pray for God to help you during the transition. He can help you make your way through it and give you better understanding about it.

WHAT'S THE BIG DEAL?

Drugs

"Come on. It's just pot," Sally pleaded, holding a small plastic bag containing two joints.

Sitting in her bedroom on a Saturday afternoon, Rebecca listened, remembering all the things she'd heard about drugs. She could hear her dad asking her to promise she'd never get into them. She could see her mother shaking her head when her cousin entered yet another drug rehab center. But did any of that really apply now? *It is just pot,* she reasoned.

"Where'd you get it?" Rebecca asked.

"My sister gave them to me. She said it's harmless—just makes you feel really relaxed. It's no big deal—not like cocaine or heroin or anything like that," Sally explained, and then added with a shrug, "Everybody does it at parties and stuff. You don't want to go to a party and freak out 'cause you've never tried it, do you?"

Although Rebecca had never considered doing drugs before, she had to admit she wondered what it was like. And Sally had a point; it *was* just marijuana. It wasn't the bad stuff. Maybe she'd give it a try. "Okay, I'll try it," she finally said.

"Cool. I didn't want to do it without my best friend," Sally said excitedly. "That's why my sister gave me two, although we can smoke the first one together."

During the next twenty minutes, Rebecca and Sally shared a joint, enjoying the euphoric sensation that washed over them. Then they felt a ravenous hunger begin to take hold of them and they raided the kitchen for munchies.

After Sally had gone home, Rebecca thought about the day. Smoking marijuana wasn't what she had expected. She'd been scared that something terrible would happen, like getting sick or freaking out. But it hadn't. She thought about it and decided that maybe Sally and her sister were right. *Maybe pot wasn't such a big deal after all,* she thought with some satisfaction.

Remembering that her parents were due home within the hour, Rebecca opened her bedroom windows, sprayed air freshener throughout the house, and rushed to clean up the kitchen. She finished just five minutes before she heard the garage door open, signaling her parents' return home after a day of running errands. Her mother walked in the house, setting grocery bags on the kitchen counter.

"Hey, Rebecca, can you help your dad bring in the rest of the bags?" her mother asked offhandedly as she began to put groceries away. "We decided to have fajitas tonight. You can invite Sally over if you want," she offered, heading to the thermostat. "Why is it so hot in here?" Then, wrinkling her nose, she asked, "And what's that smell?"

Rebecca hesitated a second before answering. Her mind raced. She'd tried so hard to make things appear and *smell* normal around the house. "Uh . . . I opened the windows for a little while this afternoon. It felt kinda stuffy in here, like it needed to be aired out. That's probably what you notice."

Her mother adjusted the temperature and looked around. "Did you clean?"

"Yeah, I picked up a little," Rebecca said nervously as she headed out the door to help her father.

After grabbing the rest of the bags, she and her father made their way into the house. As soon as her father walked into the house, he stopped. His muscles tensed. Setting the bags down, he walked through the living room and then down the hall. He stopped in front of Rebecca's bedroom, opened the door, and walked in.

Rebecca and her mother watched him. Rebecca tried to look unconcerned, but inwardly she shook. Then Rebecca's mother walked after her dad, entering Rebecca's room. A few more seconds passed and Rebecca heard mumbling coming from her room. *This is bad,* she thought desperately. *Why did I let Sally talk me into this?*

"Rebecca, come in here," her dad called.

Slowly, Rebecca walked into her room. Her mother sat on her bed with a stricken look on her face, as though she would faint any moment. Her dad stood with his back to the door, hands on his hips, looking out the window.

"Do you have something you want to say?" her father asked slowly, never turning to face her.

"No . . . well, I . . . uh . . . ," Rebecca stammered. Her mind reeled, trying to come up with the right thing to say.

As she tried to put words together, her dad spoke in a deep low tone. He meant business. "Before you say something to make this situation worse," he said, "let me encourage you to tell the truth. So I'll ask you again, do you have something to tell me?"

Shame washed over her. Rebecca dropped her gaze to the floor. In a rush, she began, "Sally and I smoked marijuana today. She said it would be okay. Not a big deal. She said it wasn't a real drug."

Her mother gasped, "Oh, Rebecca, Sally is wrong. Marijuana *is* a drug and studies show it can have long-term effects on your body, mind, and spirit." Her voice trailed off and she looked down at the floor.

Her father stood rigid. "I've seen kids in my clinic who thought the same thing about marijuana." She saw pain, disappointment, and fear on her dad's face. She knew she'd made a mistake.

"Is this the first time you've experimented with drugs? And, yes, marijuana is a drug, regardless of what Sally says. It can cause problems with memory, learning, lack of perception, and difficulty in thinking and problem solving. Research links it to respiratory problems, lung infections, and even cancer."

"Yes, I promise it's the first time I tried it. I was just curious," Rebecca admitted dejectedly, and then added, "Dad, I'll never do it again. I promise."

"I wish I could believe you, Rebecca," her father said shaking his head, "but we can't just ignore this. I love you, but at this point, I don't trust you."

Rebecca felt the weight of her choice. Over the next few hours, Rebecca and her parents sat around the dining room table and talked about the dangers of drugs. They also discussed Rebecca's punishment.

They discussed her friendship with Sally. Her father planned to call Sally's parents the next day. She wouldn't be allowed to spend time alone with Sally anymore. In fact, it would be a while before she would be allowed to stay home alone at all. And her parents decided she needed to visit their cousin at the drug treatment center so that Rebecca could hear firsthand how drug addiction starts with small steps.

By the end of the night, Rebecca was exhausted—physically, mentally, and emotionally. She had crossed over into a new place—a place she'd give anything to never have gone. Her parents didn't trust her. She had lost the trust that they had once freely given, and she had taken for granted.

As she lay down to go to sleep, she wondered how long it would take for her mom and dad to trust her again. She wondered what Sally would say once her parents knew about the drugs. Sally would probably be angry, and even that made Rebecca sad.

TRUTH UNPLUGGED:

Drugs takes you down the wrong path—away from God and everything else that's important in your life. Choose life.

Her friendship with Sally had changed too. Her parents now viewed Sally with suspicion. Although they hadn't said she and Sally couldn't be friends, she knew they would prefer that Rebecca make other friends.

Rebecca knew that she'd lost a lot that day. Some of it she could earn back, but some, she realized, was lost for good. *It really did turn out to be a big deal after all,* she thought as she desperately tried to fall asleep.

TRUTH LINK:

Dear Lord, help me to stand strong against drugs so that I'm not tempted to take them. I want to stay on the right track in my life, and I realize that drugs are not any part of Your plan. Please, give me the strength to not only make the right decisions but to also live with the consequence of my actions. Amen.

Perhaps you've heard that for every action there is a reaction.

POWER UP:

It is true in life. You make choices every day that result in good or bad consequences. Drugs bring bad consequences—plain and simple. Aside from what they do to your health, they can consume every aspect of your life. Don't let anyone convince you that they're harmless. And if you're making the decision to stop using them, know that God will always forgive you and help you. You're never too far gone for Him to stop loving you. Though your circumstances may not immediately change, He will help you face them.

NOTHING BUT THE TRUTH

G o s s i p

DOWNLOAD:

"You shall not bear false witness against your neighbor."
Exodus 20:16 NKJV

"You know what?" Sherry asked the lunch group during the first day of school. "I heard Lisa Patterson left school last year to have a baby, and she gave it up for adoption."

All at once, Sherry, Jill, Stacy, and Dana turned and stared at Lisa as she joined her friends at another table. Dana listened to what Sherry said but didn't respond. Though she wasn't a close friend with Lisa, they had worked together on the school year-book the previous fall.

To Dana, Lisa had always been one of the smart kids. If there was an A to be had on a test or a project, it was hers. But that didn't make her a nerd. In fact, she was gorgeous, funny, and well-liked—someone who was nice to everyone. Though she dated, as far as anyone knew she'd never had a serious boyfriend. Then last year she'd left school a few months early without any explanation, and now she was back, looking a few pounds heavier.

"Who was the father?" Stacy whispered to Sherry.

"Nobody knows. Maybe Jeff Long. You know they went out a few times last Christmas. Or maybe Todd Rigby from the chess club. I used to see them hanging out together in chemistry lab. Maybe something heated up a little too much in there," she joked.

Everyone laughed.

As the day wore on, Dana moved from class to class, settling into her schedule. Just before the fifth period late bell rang, she raced into anatomy class and grabbed the first available seat. Turning to see who shared her lab table, she saw Lisa smiling at her.

"Hey, Dana," she said. "I'm glad I got a good person to sit with. That'll make the research part a lot easier." Dana nodded and smiled back, thinking she had lucked out since Lisa was the best student in the class. She tried hard not to look at Lisa's belly and wondered if what Sherry has said was true.

Just then Sherry entered the class, waved, and mouthed, "Todd Rigby," forcing Dana to stifle a giggle.

As class wore on, everyone received their books and class guidelines. Lisa turned to Dana and asked, "Hey, do you want to exchange phone numbers so we can call each other if we get hung up on the homework?"

"Sure. That'd be great," Dana responded. Then hesitating, she asked, "Say, didn't you leave school early last year?"

Shifting uncomfortably in her chair, Lisa opened her notebook to arrange papers. "Uh . . . yeah, I had something to take care of."

Dana smiled and nodded. When class was over, they gathered their books and said good-bye. On the way out the door, Sherry joined Dana.

"So, did you find out anything?" she asked.

"Only that she had 'something to take care of,'" Dana simply replied.

"*Something to take care of,*" Sherry said mischievously. "I'll say. Maybe about a seven- or eight-pound something."

Over the next few weeks, Sherry continued to press Dana to find out more about Lisa's secret. "Come on," she said several times. "You'll be like Barbara Walters snooping out the biggest story of your career. I'm *sure* she was pregnant and gave her baby up. Just prove it. The public *deserves* to know the truth."

Dana wasn't so sure the public deserved to know anything, and she refused to be a part of such a vicious rumor. Even if Lisa had been pregnant, Dana didn't want to be part of her public humiliation.

The first anatomy test was scheduled four weeks into the school year. Dana rushed to class eager to look over her notes once more before the test, but glancing over at the empty seat next to her, she noticed Lisa wasn't there. In fact, Lisa missed the test altogether. After class the teacher, Mrs. Walton, asked Dana to stay for a few minutes.

"Dana, are you and Lisa close friends?" she asked.

"Not really *close*," Dana responded, somewhat puzzled by her question, "but we're friends. We study together."

"Well, I wanted to send some work home to her and thought maybe you could take it to her."

"Sure. Is she sick?" Dana asked.

Mrs. Walton looked down for a moment and then looked back at her, never answering Dana's question. "Just take her this stack, would you?" she said mildly.

After school, Dana drove over to Lisa's house. They didn't live in the same neighborhood, but Dana knew where Lisa lived. She quietly knocked on the door.

After a few seconds, Lisa opened it. Dressed in pajamas and a robe, Lisa looked awful!

"Lisa, are you okay?" Dana asked in horror. The change in her appearance was startling. She had dark circles under her eyes, and she looked pale and exhausted.

Smiling, she said, "Hey, Dana, I'm fine. Come on in."

Turning, she slowly walked back to her couch and lay down. "Have a seat," she offered.

"You look like you feel *terrible,*" Dana said, still reeling from the shock of Lisa's altered appearance. Sitting down, she asked, "Can I get you anything?"

"No, I'll be okay," she said, closing her eyes for a minute. "I just need to rest a moment. Just getting up to answer the door is a big deal for me today."

Composing herself, Dana watched her. She knew that Lisa was dealing with more than just the flu. She was really sick.

"Do you want me to leave?" Dana asked, thinking Lisa obviously needed her rest.

"No, please stay. It's nice to see a friend," Lisa said, opening her eyes. "You're probably a little shocked to see me like this, but don't worry. It's not contagious."

"What's wrong with you anyway?" Dana asked gently.

"Basically, I need a new kidney," Lisa said. "There's a big word for it, but it comes down to that. I left school early last year when I got sick. I have been on dialysis all summer, but some days it still gets the best of me. I'm on the organ donor list though. They think I may get one really soon." Then laughing, she added, "You know, there's actually a rumor going around that I had a baby last year, and that's the reason I left school early."

"Yeah, I heard that," Dana admitted.

"I'm sure the whole school has. It's no big deal though. I'd rather everyone think that than feel sorry for me and act all weird around me, ya know?" Dana smiled weakly as Lisa spoke, thinking about how big a mistake the rumor really was.

Lisa and Dana talked for about an hour. Dana promised that she wouldn't say anything about Lisa's sickness and that she'd come back to visit her in a few days if she hadn't returned to school.

A week later, Lisa still hadn't returned. Dana had kept in touch with her by phone. And true to her word, Dana kept the reason for Lisa's absence to herself.

Then one day over lunch, Sherry shocked everyone with the truth. "I heard Lisa Patterson is in the hospital. Somebody said she's getting a kidney trans-plant."

A silence fell over the group.

Dana remained quiet and continued to eat her lunch. Puzzled, Sherry looked at

TRUTH UNPLUGGED:

When you speak about someone, say only positive things. Build them up and be known as someone who believes the best of every person.

her. "You knew, didn't you?" Dana gave her a look that commu-nicated that she did. "Why didn't you tell us? We're supposed to be friends. How could you keep something like that to yourself?"

Dana slowly lowered her fork. "Because Lisa asked me not to. She knew there was a rumor going around that she had had a baby last year, when the truth was she was sick. But she'd rather have people believe the rumor than feel sorry for her. So she made me promise not to tell."

No one spoke right away. After looking around the group, each girl silently looked down at her food.

"I guess we were really wrong thinking she was pregnant, huh?" Sherry said quietly. "I feel awful."

Dana nodded. "Yeah, the rumor definitely got out of control." Then, thinking a minute, she added, "I'm going by the hospital tonight to visit her. Anyone want to join me?"

Sherry smiled and nodded. "Yeah, I'd like that. I owe her a *huge* apology."

As the lunch continued, Dana could tell that each person was lost in her own thoughts, realizing just how wrong the rumor really had been. *Maybe some good will come out of this rumor after all,* she thought.

TRUTH LINK:

Dear Lord, I have gotten caught up in spreading rumors. Please forgive me. Help me to not listen to or spread gossip. Show me when I need to walk away when people around me perpetuate rumors. Help me to be strong and stay away from it. Amen.

POWER UP:

Telling a friend something you've heard can seem like such a harmless thing, but it isn't. A false witness hurts the people you talk about, you, your reputation, and your relationship with God. Think about someone you know who spreads rumors. Is she someone you want to turn to in a crisis? God wants you to speak well of others and bring light and life into your relationships. Even if a rumor proves true, if it's not positive—building someone up and encouraging them—then it's not worth repeating.

FUZZY MEMORIES

Drinking

DOWNLOAD:

Be sober, be vigilant; because your adversary the devil walks about like a roaring lion, seeking whom he may devour.

1 Peter 5:8 NKJV

Slowly opening her eyes, Amber felt the sudden pain shoot through her head.

Bang, bang, bang.

Oh, the hammering was real. Everything seemed so bright. Slowly, with great effort, she sat up. Looking around, she realized she was at her friend Kara's house, but she didn't remember getting there. The last thing she remembered was being at Rick's party with her boyfriend, Bob. *So how did I end up here?* she wondered.

Slowly standing up, she fought to keep her balance as her head continued to spin. *What happened?* She tried to remember the night before but couldn't quite place the pieces together. She remembered having a few drinks, but she couldn't have gotten that drunk, could she? Of course, if she wasn't hungover, she didn't know what she was.

Peering out Kara's bedroom door, Amber saw no one. She slowly made her way to the bathroom. Staring at her reflection in the mirror, she couldn't believe it was her. Her face looked puffy, she had dark circles under her eyes, and her eye makeup was smeared all over. Her mouth felt dry, like she'd swallowed a bag of cotton balls. Slowly, she turned the faucet on and splashed her face. The cold water felt good. Standing back up, she noticed for the first time that her shirt wasn't buttoned correctly. The buttons were one button off. *How did that happen?*

After cleaning up as best she could, she slowly made her way to the kitchen. Kara sat at the dining room table eating breakfast. Looking up when Amber entered the room, she gave her a weary smile. "Good morning. How are you feeling?"

"Awful," Amber said flatly.

Kara nodded without any surprise. "Do you want something to eat? My parents are out running errands so you don't have to worry about them asking you questions."

Eating was the furthest thing from Amber's mind, but she knew she should get something into her stomach. She could already feel the queasiness starting. "Maybe just a piece of bread."

Kara got it for her and also brought back a glass of water. "You had a big night last night."

Though foggy, Amber could hear the coldness in Kara's voice. They were close friends, and she knew when Kara was angry about something. "What happened?" she asked cautiously.

Kara took a deep breath. "Do you want the long or the short version?" When Amber only stared at her, she began. "Well, let's see. Basically, you got plastered at Rick's party."

Amber shook her head. "I don't remember anything. How did I end up here? I went to the party with Bob."

Kara stared at her. "You really don't remember *anything?*" Amber shook her head slowly back and forth. "Well," Kara said, "you and Bob had a fight at the party. He tried to get you to stop drinking and you wouldn't. You got angry and screamed at him when he tried to stop you from doing a striptease on top of Rick's dining room table." Amber looked at her in disbelief. "But what really sealed it is when he caught you in Rick's parents' hot tub with Pete Talbot."

"Oh no!" Amber cried in shock.

Kara watched her a moment before continuing. "Amber, I don't know what you were thinking last night or what you drank, but you were out of control. You were all over Pete and a couple of other guys I'd never seen before. Bob finally left after he caught you in the hot tub. We tried to get you out of there sooner, but you were wild. I finally helped carry you home after you passed out."

Amber felt sick. How could all that have happened? How could she have drunk that much? She didn't remember any of it.

On Monday, Amber nervously walked into school. She wasn't usually a wild child. In fact, everyone had thought of her as a good, church-going girl. Sometimes she drank at parties, but it had never gotten out of hand. In fact, she'd never been drunk before. But if everything Kara had told her was true, she'd really made up for it this time.

She'd tried to call Bob a couple of times on Sunday afternoon, but she repeatedly got his voice mail. She was pretty sure he was avoiding her when he hadn't called her back. Now, seeing him in the halls, she hoped he would forgive her and they could forget the party. Walking up behind him, she said, "Bob, can we talk? I know I was a jerk at the party, but I'm really sorry. I don't know what happened. I don't even remember."

Bob turned around and looked at her in disgust. "I'll tell you what happened, Amber. You made out with half the guys there. Gave them a full show and everything."

"I'm sorry." Tears had started to well up in her eyes. "Please tell me we can get past this."

"You're kidding, right?" Bob said, looking at her as if she had the plague. "We're over. I don't ever want to see you again. I'm embarrassed that I actually dated you. Do you really think I want to date a slut from the party?" Then he turned and marched down the hallway.

Watching him go, Amber felt as if she'd been slapped. She wasn't a "slut." She was good and tame compared to most girls in school.

Turning around to make her way to class, Amber noticed several people eavesdropping. Of course they were trying to pretend like they weren't, but there were too many people clustered together, glancing her way, for them not to have heard Bob's remarks.

Throughout the morning, she noticed several of her friends avoiding her. They weren't making eye contact, and several snickered as she walked by. Later, during lunch, as she made her way to her table, one of guys from the football team jumped up and lifted his shirt, flashing her. "Come on, Amber. Show us that little dance you gave us the other night." Several people cheered and laughed as she pushed her way past him to her usual seat by Kara.

Kara watched her arrive at the table. "How's your day?" Amber shot her a sad, helpless look. Kara nodded, "I thought it might be going like that."

A few minutes later, Pete Talbot walked up to the table and slid down next to her, much too close for comfort. "Hey, Amber, there's another party this weekend. You wanna go? We can pick up where we left off, and maybe this time we won't be interrupted," he said in a seductive tone.

Amber thought she'd be sick.

Pete Talbot was the sleaziest guy in school. He was forever bragging about how girls fell at his feet. Now, Amber realized she had joined his list. Feeling the walls close in, she shoved Pete away and raced out of the school. She couldn't breathe as sobs overwhelmed her, threatening to choke all the air out of her lungs. Clinging to a pillar just outside the school entrance, Amber wept.

Feeling a hand on her shoulder, she turned and found Kara. Gently, Kara rubbed her back, letting her cry and get it all out. When Amber had calmed down, she said, "Give everyone a few weeks and this is going to be nothing but a bad memory."

Amber shook her head back and forth. "How could this have happened? I didn't mean for it to happen."

"You drank, Amber. It's as simple as that." Kara stated matter-of-factly. "You thought you could control it, but once you had a couple drinks in you, your judgment went out the window."

 **TRUTH UNPLUGGED:**

Don't let anyone—even your friends—talk you into drinking alcohol. Take a stand against it.

"Well, that'll never happen again. I'm never going to drink again. I'm so humiliated," Amber sobbed.

"I know. Honestly, you'll get though this," Kara said calmly. "And the good news is, you'll never make this mistake again. God will forgive you, and so will your good friends, like me," she said with a comical smile, causing Amber to grin through her tears.

God, please forgive me, she prayed. *I promise I'll never drink again.* Amber prayed inwardly as a few more tears escaped her eyes. Then, hearing the bell signaling the end of lunch, she dried her eyes and walked back into the school with Kara. Amber wasn't sure how she would face all the teasing and gossip, but she knew she'd just have to take it one step at a time.

TRUTH LINK:

Dear Lord, I don't want to drink, but there are a lot of people that I know—even close friends—who do. Please give me the strength to stand up for what I believe. Help me to have the strength to say no when someone offers me alcohol. Amen.

POWER UP:

You may have close friends who think it's fun to drink and get drunk. But drinking can kill you. Don't become trapped into thinking, **THAT'LL NEVER HAPPEN TO ME**. Alcohol consumption—a lethal amount in the bloodstream has caused the death of many teens. Many are also killed each year from drunk driving or the actions of those who are under the influence of alcohol. It can impair your judgement. Don't allow your friends to pressure you into making a detrimental, life-altering mistake. If you feel trapped, call for help from friends or parents. It's difficult to stand up to others and say no, but don't follow the group. Take a stand; it may just save your life.

THE COURAGE TO RUN

Courage

"Lilly, I really appreciate all your hard work on the Adopt-a-Family project. It was a bigger success than ever before. Have you thought about running for student council president next month? You really have a way of rallying people to follow your lead."

"Wow, thanks, Dr. Denton. Umm no, I haven't thought about running for student council. I don't really think I'm cut out for it. Getting people involved in the Adopt-a-Family project was easy. I don't really think it was anything I did."

"Oh, I think you underestimate yourself," Dr. Denton said. "You really motivated the students to get behind that project. You know, inspiring people is a sign of a good leader. Just think about running, okay? I think you'd do a great job."

Lilly promised she would and then left the principal's office to meet her best friend, Karyn, for lunch.

He must be kidding, she thought skeptically as she walked down the hallway. *I'm not student council president material.*

After getting her lunch, she sat down across from Karyn at their usual table. Karyn was trying to rub paint off of her arm. A true artist, Karyn lived to paint, sculpt, and draw. She always spent time before and after school in the art studio. "How'd your meeting go with Dr. Denton?" she asked. "Was he impressed with how well the Adopt-a-Family project went?"

"Yeah, he was impressed," Lilly said, and then offhandedly added, "He even thinks I should run for student council president. Isn't that funny?"

Karyn stopped rubbing her arm and stared wide-eyed at Lilly. "That's an awesome idea, Lil! Wow! You should!"

Lilly scowled at her. "Quit joking around. I couldn't run for student council president."

"Why not?"

"Oh, come on, like I'd even have a chance. I've never even considered it before. I hate giving speeches. And I'm not popular enough."

"What are you talking about? Lilly, people love you! And so what if you have to give a few speeches? You can do that. You're just scared."

"Whatever. Can we talk about something else?"

Karyn conceded, but Lilly knew she wouldn't give up that easily.

Truthfully, Lilly wasn't sure Karyn was wrong. She was scared. What if she lost? What if she made a fool out of herself during the speech and threw up in front of everyone? Ugh! She wouldn't be able to show her face again at school. No, it was just easier to forget the whole thing.

But then again, the thought of being student council president was interesting. She could set up some worthwhile volunteer activities for the students and make homecoming week really festive. And she could work with the administration on senior privileges—parking, the senior trip, and college prep programs. *That would be fun,* she thought.

After lunch, Lilly made her way to English. The class was studying Ernest Hemingway's *The Old Man and the Sea.* After taking her seat, her teacher, Mrs. Thornton, called the roll and took her place at the front of the class. "Okay everyone, let's talk about *The Old Man and the Sea.* You should have finished reading it last night. So what did you think?"

No one answered.

Mrs. Thornton continued, "Come on, tell me. Here we have this Cuban fisherman who battles this huge fish for what seems like an eternity. After finally catching the fish, he tries to haul it all the way back home, just to have it eaten by sharks along the way. Was it worth his trouble?

TRUTH UNPLUGGED:

You have God-given gifts and talents in you. Have the courage to use them.

At first, no one answered. Then, one of the football players piped up, "I think he should have saved himself some time and hiked down to Long John Silver's."

Everyone laughed.

"Okay, that actually brings up a good point," Mrs. Thornton continued. "Why'd he do it? He could have packed it in and gone home. Why'd he stick with it?"

Lilly raised her hand, "I think he did it to prove to himself that he could. He wanted respect—not just from the other fishermen, but also from himself."

Mrs. Thornton smiled and nodded, "That's a possibility. Do you think it was worth his effort?"

"Yes, I do," Lilly answered. "He not only gained self-respect for beating the fish, but also for having the courage to make the effort."

Mrs. Thornton smiled. "So the fact that the fish was eaten by sharks didn't matter?

Lilly thought about it a second, tilting her head to the side in contemplation. "No, I mean, I'm sure he would have liked to have had it, but I think he was just happy to know he tried and beat the fish."

Just then, Lilly thought of her own dilemma. She reflected on her own "big fish"—the student council presidency. If she was honest with herself, she had to admit that she really wanted to be president, but did she have the courage to run? Could she face it if she lost? But worse than running, Lilly wondered if she could face it if she refused to try? Throughout the rest of class, Lilly tried to listen but couldn't stop thinking about running for president. By the end of class, she knew what she had to do. She had to try.

Later that afternoon, she returned to Dr. Denton's office to ask for the candidacy forms. He was pleased she had taken his advice and decided to run. She told him about some of the things she hoped to use as campaign issues. Impressed by her initiative, he offered to look over her campaign speech and make recommendations before she gave it. As they talked, she became more and more excited about running.

After leaving Dr. Denton's office, Lilly made her way to the art studio to look for Karyn. She figured Karyn should be the first person she told about her decision. Based on their conversation at lunch, she knew Karyn would be ecstatic. As she entered, she saw Karyn intensely painting. After Lilly cleared her throat, Karyn looked up and smiled.

"I have something to tell you," Lilly began. "I've decided to run for student council president, and I need a campaign manager."

"All right!" Karyn squealed. "Well, as the first order of business as your campaign manager, I need your opinion. What do you think of this poster?" She pointed at the artwork she had been painting.

Lilly moved closer to Karyn to take a look. On the easel, Karyn had painted a pink and white lily in the background with the words "Pick Lilly for President" inscribed in purple at the top and bottom.

"You are too much, Karyn. How did you know I'd run?" Lilly laughingly asked.

Karyn smiled. "Are you kidding? You're way too strong to pass up a challenge like this, Lilly—too courageous to chicken out.

For the rest of the afternoon, Lilly and Karyn planned Lilly's presidency campaign. They decided on her running mate for vice president, the issues she would work on, and her campaign artwork. With each passing moment, Lilly's courage grew. She knew that she still had a tough battle ahead, but she wasn't afraid. She knew she was going to give it her best, and as long as she did that, she felt confident that she'd be a winner, no matter the outcome.

TRUTH LINK:

Dear Lord, I know You've given me talents and abilities, and I want to use them for You. Help me to have the courage to do the things that You want me to do and not become nervous or afraid. Thank You for the courage to face anything that comes my way. Amen.

POWER UP:

God wants you to have the courage to use the talents and abilities He has given you. Maybe you're good at sports or mathematics. Or perhaps you have the ability to encourage and motivate others. Whatever your talents are, have the courage to use them. Although you may be afraid or nervous, don't let that stop you from doing the things God wants you to do. When He asks you to do it, He gives you the faith and courage to pursue it.

NOT MY PROBLEM

Eating Disorders

DOWNLOAD:

What happens when we live God's way? He brings gifts into our lives, much the same way that fruit appears in an orchard—things like affection for others, exuberance about life, serenity. We develop a willingness to stick with things, a sense of compassion in the heart, and a conviction that a basic holiness permeates things and people. Galatians 5:22 THE MESSAGE

Wendi *loved* pep rallies. She loved hearing the band play, seeing the screaming pep club jump up and down, and rooting for the football team as they took the floor. Getting into the spirit of things was easy.

She especially enjoyed watching the cheerleaders tumble through the air. She had been a cheerleader the previous two years, but after breaking her ankle at cheerleading camp, she had decided to hang up her pom-poms.

Sometimes she missed the camaraderie of the squad. Although she had hoped to remain close to her cheerleader friends, they had inevitably drifted apart. She wasn't angry about it. In fact, she understood. It was just hard to remain in the inner circle when everyone on the squad went to camp together, practiced for several hours a day, and performed at games and competitions.

Fortunately, she had made other close friends at school and church. It had taken her awhile to find her place now that she wasn't a cheerleader. Now, she was just one of the crowd. She'd even begun to enjoy it. She had joined the drama club and school vocal ensemble. Her friends might not be the most popular in school, but they were fun, dramatic, and talented.

The school day ended when the pep rally was over. Wendi hung around and talked to a few friends while almost everyone else filtered out and made their way home. As a last-minute errand, she went to the girls' locker room to retrieve her dirty gym clothes. Hearing someone vomiting in one of the bathroom stalls stopped her in her tracks. After a second or two, she continued to her locker and hoped that the person was all right. Hearing the person exit the bathroom, she turned and saw it was Veronica, one of her friends from the cheerleading squad.

"Hey, Ron, are you okay?" Wendi asked with concern.

Startled, Veronica stopped. "Oh, hey, Wendi. Sure, I'm fine. I just ate something that didn't agree with me. See ya later." She turned and quickly left.

Wendi paused.

While on the squad, Wendi and Veronica had been close friends. Once, Veronica had admitted that she sometimes threw up after she ate too much. It had always shocked Wendi to think Veronica resorted to that. Veronica was the girl everyone else wanted to be. She was beautiful, popular, smart, and had a great family. Judging from the outside, her life was perfect.

Wendi gathered her clothes and headed home, continuing to think about Veronica. *Maybe she was overreacting. Maybe Veronica had eaten something that didn't agree with her. And so what if she sometimes threw up after she ate? It didn't necessarily mean she had an eating disorder, did it? And even if Veronica had the eating disorder bulimia, and she binged and then purged her food, was it really her place to say anything?*

Over the weekend, Wendi continued to wonder about Veronica. Though she tried to put it out of her mind, she couldn't let it go. She even looked up bulimia on the Internet. Since she and Veronica weren't close anymore, she didn't know Veronica's eating patterns, but what she did find out was that if Veronica was bulimic, she was battling something extremely dangerous and needed help.

On Monday, Wendi looked for Veronica during lunch period. She found her sitting with a few other cheerleaders.

"Hey, Ron. How was your weekend?" she asked.

Veronica looked up and smiled. "Oh, hi, Wendi. It was great. We won Friday night, which always makes for a great weekend."

Looking around, Wendi noticed that Veronica was the only one at the table not eating. "Aren't you having lunch?"

"Oh, no," she said quickly, then added, "I've already eaten."

They talked a few more minutes, and then Wendi left to join her regular group. She wasn't any closer to discovering whether Veronica was in trouble or not. Again, she tried to dismiss the whole idea that it was her business.

The next day, she decided to talk to Veronica about her suspicion. She just couldn't take agonizing over it anymore. Though she knew Veronica might either think she was crazy or never speak to her again, she had to take the chance. After her last class, she began to search all over school. She knew cheerleading practice started thirty minutes after classes finished, so she didn't have much time. First, she walked the halls. Then she checked the cafeteria, library, and finally the gym. *Lord, help me find her,* Wendi prayed.

Just when she was about to give up, she entered the girls' locker room. She stopped. The sound of someone vomiting was unmistakable. Quietly walking back to the stalls, she waited. Within a couple of minutes the stall door opened and Veronica walked out.

"Hey, Ron," Wendi said.

"What do you want?" Veronica said suspiciously.

"I just want to talk to you. I had a funny feeling last Friday when I heard you throwing up in here after the pep rally. I've thought about it all weekend," Wendi explained.

"So. It's none of your business," Veronica said defensively.

"I keep telling myself the same thing, but the thing is, I care. And if you're in trouble, I can't ignore it," Wendi said and then continued. "Look, we were good friends at one time.

TRUTH UNPLUGGED:

God wants to use you to show His compassion to people who are hurting.

And if you're doing what I think you're doing—binging and purging—you have to get help. It's nothing to play around with."

Veronica listened with an irritated look on her face. Her face softened as Wendi spoke, then she quietly admitted, "I don't know how to stop. I used to be able to control it, but now . . . You probably think I'm really screwed up, don't you?"

"No, I just think you need help. I found a place here in town that treats bulimia, and I'll even go with you, if you want," Wendi offered.

Veronica seemed to consider Wendi's offer. "But what if people find out?"

"Isn't it more important to be free from this? Don't think about what people may or may not think. I'm not going to tell any of the kids at school," she paused, wondering how to phrase her next statement, "but I *will* tell your parents or a school counselor."

"You'd tell?" Veronica cried.

Wendi nodded, inwardly shaking.

After a few seconds of hesitation, Veronica asked, "You'd really go with me?"

"Yeah, I would."

Veronica missed cheerleading practice, and she and Wendi spent the next few hours talking. Veronica told her how scared she was and even admitted that she was relieved someone finally knew. Then they prayed. Wendi wasn't sure what would happen next, but she was glad Veronica agreed to get help.

Later that night, after Wendi got home, she made Veronica's appointment for the next day, and then reached for her Bible. Though she knew she didn't have the answers to Veronica's problem, she knew God did. *Maybe Veronica isn't my responsibility,* Wendi thought, but then again, maybe God had made Veronica her responsibility when He let her know what was happening. As she flipped through her Bible, Wendi felt a sense of peace knowing that she had been in the right place at the right time.

TRUTH LINK:

Dear Lord, help me to be compassionate toward other people. I don't want to ignore someone who is suffering. I want to be someone You use to help people in need. Show me the steps to take to help someone who is hurting. Amen.

POWER UP:

Have you ever known someone with an eating disorder—anorexia or bulimia—but not known what to do? Have you ever tried to convince yourself that their pain is none of your concern? It's easy to do. It's easy to convince yourself not to get involved in someone's life. You may be unsure of how they'll react, or you may not know what to say. But God can still use you. Through you, He can show His compassion and love to others. He wants them to know He's concerned about their pain and has the answer to their problems. So if you know someone who is battling an eating disorder, don't be too quick to dismiss your role in their situation. When you're moved by compassion for them, you can be God's hands in their life.

STICK WITH IT

Diligence

DOWNLOAD:

Easy come, easy go, but steady diligence pays off.

Proverbs 13:11 THE MESSAGE

"Mary, I want to talk to you about your summer plans," her dad said as they sat down to dinner.

"But it's only March. I don't know what I'm going to do yet."

"Well, that's why I want to talk to you about it now. You're turning sixteen in August, and you mentioned that you want a car. You need to think about getting a job to earn money for it."

Mary stopped eating and stared at her dad. "I thought I was getting Mom's car."

"Well, your mom and I have talked about it, and we've decided that you need to work for your vehicle. We know you're able to drive at sixteen, but we would feel better about your buying a vehicle with money that you earned rather than having one we simply gave you. We think you'll appreciate it more," her dad explained.

Mary was shocked and irritated that her parents had decided she couldn't have her mom's Honda Civic. She'd already planned to have it repainted and loaded with a new multiple CD changer. Disappointed, she sulked, pushing the remains of her dinner around her plate.

"Well, that's why I wanted to talk to you about it now. One of the guys I work with has a daughter who's a counselor at a nearby summer camp. There are two summer sessions—one in June and the other in July. You'd stay at the camp with the kids. The pay isn't great, but considering you wouldn't have to find transportation to and from work or be tempted to spend your earnings at the mall, you could have a pretty good amount saved by the end of the summer."

"It doesn't sound like much fun," Mary said.

"I don't think hanging out with little kids for a summer sounds so bad," her dad encouraged. "You'll get to take them swimming and roast marshmallows and other things you do at camp. Of course, you don't have to do it. But if you don't, you'll have to think of something else. Whatever you decide, you need to make enough money to pay for the car and your gas. You mother and I will cover your insurance."

Mary hadn't even thought about what she'd do over summer vacation. She sure hadn't considered working all summer—especially with little kids. She knew that this was what her father called a defining moment in her life—working to earn money for her first car. Mary knew she didn't have to have a car, but having her parents take her to school each day wasn't the greatest thing in the world, and riding the school bus was definitely out of the question. So she had no choice—she had to find a job.

For the next few days, Mary tried to think of alternatives to being a kids' camp counselor, but she couldn't come up with anything that was steady enough and didn't require her to get a ride to work every day. Her parents' schedules were busy enough. They couldn't transport her to and from work at random hours.

Although she was disappointed that she wouldn't be able to see her friends all summer, she decided to submit her application for camp counselor.

At the end of April, after a phone interview and an in-person interview with the camp director, she was hired. Over the next month, she gathered all the stuff she needed—bug repellant, sunscreen, sunglasses, bathing suit, backpack, allergy medicine. . . . On June 1st her parents dropped her off at the camp. Her mother hugged her fiercely and made her promise to call or write at least once a week. Her dad hugged her, saying, "You're going to have a great time, sweetheart. I'm really proud of you for doing this. And if you stick with it, you'll have the reward of owning your first car. Trust me, it'll be worth it."

Mary tried to smile, but she felt disheartened. *Maybe I don't really need a car after all,* she reasoned and then thought, *If I really hate it here, I can always quit.*

Joining the other counselors for orientation, she learned the location of her cabin and her duties. She discovered that she would share a cabin with one other counselor. Together, they would be responsible for twenty girls each session.

As the camp director talked about the rules and schedule, Mary looked around. There were close to fifty counselors in the room—boys and girls who were around her age. She recognized a few faces from school but didn't really know anyone. *What have I gotten myself into?* she wondered. *Lord, give me strength.*

After the meeting ended, an athletic girl who looked a few years older than Mary came over. "Hey, my name's Rita. We're co-counselors together. This your first time?"

"Yeah, this is my first time."

"Well, don't worry, this is my third year. Trust me, we're gonna have a blast," she beamed. "Every summer I can't wait to get back to these kids."

Though initially skeptical, Mary quickly discovered how much fun and how challenging her role as a camp counselor could be. Thankfully, she had Rita to show her the ropes. Rita, who was studying to be an elementary gym teacher, took her role very seriously. She'd constantly remind Mary to "stick with it." If a child had a hard day dealing with homesickness, Rita would tell Mary to "stick with it" until the kid was laughing. If kids refused to do what they were supposed to do, Rita encouraged Mary to "stick with it" until they came around and did what they were supposed to do.

At the end of the two months, Mary was surprised to discover that she was sad to leave. It had been one of the best summers of her life. It hadn't been easy, but she'd finally learned to just "stick with it." In the end, she'd gained a lot. She now had a good start on her car savings, and she'd learned that she really enjoyed working with children.

> ## TRUTH UNPLUGGED:
>
> Make the decision to be diligent—to never give up—in your family, school, relationships, and job. The reward will be well worth the effort.

Two months later, Mary turned sixteen, received her driver's license, and bought her first vehicle. She had to admit that paying for it with her own money felt good. She didn't have enough money to upgrade the speakers or have it repainted, but Mary didn't mind. She was proud of it anyway.

Instead of buying a car, she'd opted for a small truck. It was the perfect vehicle to help with her new after-school job at the local community center. She was in charge of transporting inner tubes when she took kids swimming at the lake. Balancing school, church, friends, and work wasn't easy, but she discovered that if she just "stuck with it" she could make it happen. And the reward made the effort well worth it.

TRUTH LINK:

Dear Lord, I have something I need to do, but right now, it seems too hard to achieve it. I know I need to press forward and keep working toward my goal, but it would be easier to give up. Help me to be diligent. I want to become someone who is diligent in big things and small things, but I recognize that I need Your help. Amen.

POWER UP:

Have you ever thought about giving up and quitting something important? A job? School? A friendship? Or do you have a goal that seems so far away that you can't imagine attaining it, like buying a car or going to college? You will always have opportunities to give up when things get hard or when goals seem too difficult to achieve, but don't do it. Make the decision to stick with it—be diligent. When you finally accomplish your goal, you'll discover just how rewarding it is because you worked so hard for it.

A MISSED FRIENDSHIP

Cliques

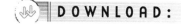

DOWNLOAD:

So, chosen by God for this new life of love, dress in the wardrobe God picked out for you: compassion, kindness, humility, quiet strength, discipline.

Colossians 3:12 THE MESSAGE

"Who is *she?*" Paula hissed. "And *what* is she doing at our table?"

"She's new. Her name's Mandy, and she's in my geometry class," Kaitlyn said.

"Well, someone needs to give her a clue. She's not welcome at our table," Paula said in disgust. "And maybe she needs to go shopping because her clothes are awful. She needs to lose the whole grunge look, or whatever look she's going for. It doesn't work."

A second later, Paula dropped her tray on the table a few feet away from Mandy and turned to glare at her. Mandy nervously looked from Paula to Kaitlyn.

As the rest of their friends arrived, Paula made it clear that Mandy had sat in the wrong place. Just loud enough for Mandy to overhear, she said, "Sorry about the lack of room, everyone. There's a little less room today since we have a squatter. I'm *sure* it won't happen tomorrow." Then she glanced down at Mandy and gave her a sarcastic smile.

Though Kaitlyn was uncomfortable with Paula's cruel behavior, she had to admit that she wasn't happy with a newcomer sitting at their table. *At least Paula has the nerve to say something,* she thought to herself. And she agreed that Mandy's clothes were shabby compared to everyone else's. She just didn't fit in, and as Mandy would soon discover, fitting in was very important at Central High School.

The next day, Kaitlyn arrived at geometry class and found Mandy in the only empty seat in the room—right next to hers.

The class begun to study a new series of theorems that Kaitlyn struggled to learn. Math had never been her strongest subject and now she feared she was in trouble. She had only scored a 70 percent on the first test and now the second one was right around the corner.

"Mandy, I see you've already covered this part and scored high on it, so this will be a review for you," Mr. Garrett said just before beginning class.

Mandy smiled and nodded in agreement.

Ugh! Kaitlyn thought. *So, she's smart. Well, she certainly isn't rich, judging from her raggedy clothes.*

At the end of class, Paula waited outside for Kaitlyn. As Mandy walked by them, Paula rolled her eyes and said in a not-so-quiet voice, "She really needs to get new clothes. Where does she buy hers anyway, the Salvation Army? I would die if I had to wear that."

Again, Kaitlyn laughed in agreement. Mandy would just have to deal with it. She had just made a bad impression on her first day, and she wasn't going to get a second chance.

Over the next couple of weeks, Kaitlyn concentrated as hard as she could on learning geometry. On the second test, she'd only scored a 65 percent. After all her studying, her grades were going down, not up. She tried to read the chapters several times, but she found it to be a waste of time since she didn't understand what she was reading. She tried doing extra homework, which still didn't help. Nothing she tried worked. She was definitely in trouble and her teacher, Mr. Garrett, knew it too.

"Kaitlyn, would you be open to having someone tutor you in geometry? I just think you need some extra help with the material," Mr. Garrett said one day after class.

"I guess so. It can't hurt. I'm not getting it on my own, that's for sure," Kaitlyn responded.

"Good. I've asked Mandy if she would be willing to help you. She said she would. She's got the highest grade in any of my classes. She'll meet you tomorrow in the library after school."

Kaitlyn couldn't believe what she was hearing. She didn't want to accept help from a loser like Mandy. *Ugh! How could I even be seen with her? What will my friends say?* Kaitlyn wondered.

Unable to come up with a quick excuse, Kaitlyn agreed to meet Mandy for geometry tutoring the next day. When she walked into the library, Mandy was already there with books and index cards spread out all around her.

"Hey," Kaitlyn said as she arrived.

Mandy glanced at her. Then she smiled and responded, "Hi, Kaitlyn. Have a seat. We can get started. My dad's picking me up in an hour."

Over the next hour, Mandy took Kaitlyn through the last few chapters their class had studied, spending extra time on the difficult sections. By the end of the hour, Kaitlyn had a better grasp on geometry than ever before. Though she felt she couldn't ace it, at least she knew what she was looking at.

Just before she left, Mandy handed Kaitlyn a stack of index cards, "Here, I made these flash cards for you. They have the theorems and rules on them. On one side is the name or question and the answer is on the back. It may seem juvenile, but it really does work. That's how I study. Do you want to meet on Thursday to go over this week's work?"

Kaitlyn agreed to meet again on Thursday, and then they went their separate ways. Kaitlyn couldn't get over how helpful and nice Mandy had been to her, even though Kaitlyn and her friends had been so mean.

On Thursday, she couldn't stand it anymore. Sitting across from Mandy studying geometry, she asked, "Why are you helping me? I've never gone out of my way to be nice to you."

Mandy looked at her and responded, "No, you haven't. But I'm not like you. I try to believe the best of people and respect everyone."

Kaitlyn's face burned with embarrassment. She really had been cruel. Although she hadn't been the one to actually *say* the nasty things to Mandy, she had still been a part of the cruelty. She had talked about her behind her back, and she'd laughed when Paula had said spiteful things.

"I'm sorry that we've been so mean to you. You sat at our table that day without asking, and you look so different. We just . . . well, you just didn't make a very good first impression," Kaitlyn reasoned.

"I didn't know it was *your* table. It was my first day. And as for my looking different, so what? My dad lost his job last year and we had to move here so he could find another one. And, yes, I have bought some of my clothes from second-hand stores, but that doesn't make me a loser. You may look down on me because of the way I look, but honestly, I feel sorry for you. Look, I agreed to help you because you need it and because Mr. Garrett asked me to, but why don't we call it a day?" Mandy said as she quickly packed her books and left.

Kaitlyn sat at the table, stunned. She felt so ashamed. Everything Mandy had said was true. She and her friends had been unfair. They'd judged her and been malicious. *Mandy had never deserved any of it,* she reasoned.

The next day in geometry class, Kaitlyn approached Mandy. "Mandy, I've been thinking about what you said yesterday and I'm sorry. My friends and I *have* been mean to you and you didn't deserve it. I don't know if you can forgive me, but if you can, maybe we can hang out after school sometime. There are some really fun places in town that you may not have visited yet."

Mandy thought about it a minute and then asked, "Won't your friends mind your hanging out with me?"

"At first maybe, but they'll come around," Kaitlyn admitted. "Anyway, I'm not worried about what they'll say."

TRUTH UNPLUGGED:

Show kindness to everyone you meet—regardless of how they look or act.

Mandy laughed, "Maybe you should be; they can be pretty ruthless."

"You let me deal with them. Trust me, they'll leave you alone from now on," Kaitlyn smiled back.

In the next few minutes before class, Kaitlyn invited Mandy to go swimming with her church youth group the following weekend. Though they had quite a way to go, Kaitlyn was confident that in time she and Mandy could become good friends.

TRUTH LINK:

Dear Lord, I need Your help to show kindness to people. Sometimes I judge them or treat them cruelly. I want to treat them the way You would have me treat them, but I need Your help. I need You to remind me and show me when I'm not treating them with kindness. I want to stop and listen to You. As for the people I've been rude to, please forgive me and show me how I can make it up to them. Amen.

POWER UP:

Treating people with kindness may seem effortless, but sometimes it's easier to lash out, to respond harshly to someone when you feel threatened, when you prejudge them, or even when you're tired and stressed. Your initial response—or your friends' initial response—can cut them with words, but as you show kindness to others, kindness **WILL** return to you. Sure, there will always be those people who are rude, but when that happens, take it to God. Ask Him to show you how to respond. Then forgive and pray for them. Don't dwell on the malicious things someone says to you. Remind yourself of special people in your life. Forgiving and praying for someone isn't always easy, but as you show kindness to others, you will receive kindness in your life.

HER BROTHER'S SECRET

Joy

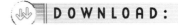

DOWNLOAD:

This day is holy to God. Don't feel bad. The joy of GOD is your strength. Nehemiah 8:10 THE MESSAGE

Andrea walked in the front door of her home and heard laughter. In the living room, she found her twin brother, Alex, laughing hysterically at a Steve Martin movie. Dropping her backpack onto the living room floor, she stormed into the kitchen to fix an after-school snack.

She couldn't understand how he could be so calm and nonchalant. Four weeks ago, their parents had told them they were getting a divorce. Since Dad had moved out, they rarely saw him, and their mom was never home. It seemed she was always at work, the lawyer's office, or at church. Andrea and Alex weren't sure where they were going to live since their mom had said they'd probably have to sell their house. They didn't even know if they would find another house in their school district.

Andrea felt as if everything was falling apart. She was angry and hurt. She threw herself into school activities to avoid coming home. She'd always enjoyed working on the yearbook, but now she spent twice as much time as anyone else on it. People had even begun to joke that she was the yearbook's "one man show."

Her brother, on the other hand, acted like nothing was wrong. In fact, he acted goofier than ever. He'd always loved comedy. In fact, his dream was to be the next big stand-up comedian. He watched funny movies, stand-up comedians, and was even enrolled in drama class in school so he could learn "comedic timing," as he put it. Andrea and he were on opposite ends of the spectrum. She couldn't hide her anger and hurt, and he didn't seem to care.

"Hey, Andi, do we have any Doritos left? I'm hungry," he asked, walking into the kitchen and opening the pantry.

"How can you do that?" she snapped.

"Do what? Eat Doritos?" he asked with a smirk as he continued to search the pantry.

"No, act like nothing's wrong. Mom and Dad are getting a divorce. We might have to move and change schools, and you act like everything's normal. In fact, you act happy. I don't get it. Don't you *care?*" Andrea's voice had risen to a roar. She was angry and tired of being the only one who seemed to have a clue about what was happening.

Alex stopped and closed the pantry. He turned to look at her, his face filled with hurt. It was the first time Andrea had seen him show anything close to sadness over their situation. "Look, Andi, I know what's happening. Trust me, I *know* what's happening. But I'm just trying to deal with it differently than you. I'm trying to find some joy in my life right now instead of wallowing in anger and self-pity," he said.

"First of all, I am *not* wallowing. Second, I don't see joy in any of this," she said, glaring at him.

Shrugging, Alex walked out of the kitchen, back to the living room, and turned the movie back on.

Andrea stood there fuming. *How dare he act so superior,* she thought.

Stalking though the living room, she grabbed her backpack and ran to her bedroom. Throwing herself across her bed, she cried like she had many times in the last few weeks. She just didn't know what to do. *Why couldn't her parents work things out? Why did they have to just give up and tear their family apart? Why did Alex have to be the one handling it so well while she was left feeling like a mess?*

She cried so hard she almost didn't hear the knock on her door. "Andi?" Alex called. "Can I come in?"

She didn't answer.

"Come on, Andi. Let me in. *Please!*" he called again.

TRUTH UNPLUGGED:

You can have the joy of the Lord in your life every moment of every day.

Without saying a word, Andrea crawled off her bed, walked to the door, and opened it. Then turning, she got back on her bed and hugged one of her throw pillows. Wearily, she watched Alex enter and sit down.

Looking at her, he said, "I'm sorry, Andi. I didn't mean to accuse you of wallowing. I just . . . I can just tell you're having a hard time, and I know I can't really help you. I feel like I'm barely able to keep my own head above water, ya know? That's why I pray every day for God's strength and joy. That's why I watch funny movies and try to laugh as much as possible."

"You seem like everything's no big deal. I feel like I'm the only one who cares about what's happening," Andrea said, her voice shaking.

"No, you're not the only one. I care. I just try to remember that I can't change what's happening. I can't make Mom and Dad stay together. All I can do is pray and try to stay happy—regardless of what else is happening."

"What do you pray? I've tried to pray, and I don't know what to ask for other than for God to make Mom and Dad change their minds," Andrea said in earnest.

"I pray for that and, like the Bible says, I pray that 'the joy of the Lord will be my strength.' That's all I know to do. And ya know what? It's working. I really feel stronger and happier," he said simply.

For the next few minutes, Andrea and Alex continued to talk about everything. For the first time since their parents announced their divorce, Andrea had someone to talk to, and she had some idea of what she could do. After they talked, they prayed. Alex prayed first and then Andrea joined in. Together, they prayed for their parents to work out their problems. They prayed for each other, asking that they would have joy and peace and strength regardless of what happened.

After they finished, they returned to the living room, ordered a pizza, and started a new movie—a funny Jackie Chan movie. Though Andrea always loved Jackie Chan flicks, she especially loved this one, this time, because she didn't have the weight of the world on her shoulders. She had finally discovered her brother's secret!

TRUTH LINK:

Dear Lord, I want Your joy to be my strength every day—not just when things are going well, but even when they aren't. I want to have Your joy with me wherever I go and during whatever I face. Please show me how to have it in my life. Amen.

Have you ever thought that some people are just born happy

POWER UP:

while others aren't? Well, although it comes more easily to some, that doesn't mean you can't be joyful every day. You can. By praying and reading your Bible, you can have the joy of the Lord too. As you turn to Him, He will help you see life from His perspective when things go wrong, and He will rejoice with you when things go right. And best of all, you'll realize that you don't have to handle everything on your own because He's right there with you.

SECOND-STRING PLAN

Pride

DOWNLOAD:

First pride, then the crash—the bigger the ego, the harder the fall. Proverbs 16:18 THE MESSAGE

This is going to be a great year! Shannon thought as she drove to school with her sister Lacy. It was the first day of her senior year. She had had a fun summer working as a lifeguard at the public pool. She had made enough money to purchase a cute car. She had a hot boyfriend, and she was all set to be the starting center on the girls' basketball team. Since the team had made it to the state finals the previous year, an offer for a college basketball scholarship was almost a sure thing. She was set for a great finale to her high school years.

"You look smug," Lacy said, eyeing her suspiciously. "What's up?"

"Nothing," she said. "I was just thinking of how great this year is going to be."

"Oh brother, my sister the campus diva. The nightmare has already begun," Lacy said, rolling her eyes. "Just remember, I knew you when you were ten and covered with chicken pox. So don't get too high and mighty."

Shannon rolled her eyes at Lacy before pulling into the school parking lot. Just then she saw Max, her boyfriend, waiting for her. They had known each other for years, but last year, he had really grown up. Most of last year he had dated Cynthia Henderson, but when they had broken up, Shannon was waiting. After a few well-timed compliments and several casual but completely planned encounters, he had asked her out. Their first date was the beginning of the summer, and they had been together ever since.

Everyone said they looked great together. He wasn't a genius, but Max certainly could be a Calvin Klein model. And many people told Shannon she could be related to Julia Roberts with her long, curly auburn hair. To Shannon, they were the perfect couple.

"Hey, babe. I'm glad you're here," Max said casually as Shannon approached him. "It'll be good for us to make our senior year entrance together. Of course, everyone knows we're together, but if we walk in together, we'll own the school this year."

Lacy walked between them, turned to Shannon, and rolled her eyes. "Oh brother," she said under her breath.

Throughout the day, Shannon was more and more convinced that this year would be the best. Many people complimented her tan and her car, and her classes would be a breeze since she'd finished her tough classes the previous year. All she had left was basketball.

After changing and making her way to the court, Shannon noticed a few new faces. The coach talked to one in particular, a new player named Debra Wilson, who had transferred in from the school across town. She had played the center position there. Shannon and Debra were now vying for the same position, but Shannon wasn't nervous. As far as she was concerned, she was a shoo-in for center.

"Shannon, can you come over here?" Coach Yancy asked. "You know Debra Wilson."

Shannon and Debra shook hands.

Coach Yancy continued, "Since you're both used to playing center, I want to take a look at you both. I'm really glad that we're going to have two strong centers, but as you know, only one of you will be first-string. You're both important to the team so don't get nervous. There's going to be plenty of playing time for both of you. After warm-up, you'll each run a few plays."

As the week progressed, Coach Yancy continued to watch Shannon and Debra. Shannon realized that Debra was more competition than she'd originally thought. As far as Shannon could tell, they were about even. Both could shoot well, but Debra could make the three-pointers and free throws better. Shannon, on the other hand, was faster on her feet and played great defense.

At the end of practice on Friday, Coach Yancy posted the team roster, showing who had made which position. Shannon looked for her name under center. First-string Debra Wilson. Second-string Shannon Chapman. Shannon couldn't believe her eyes. *How could the coach place me as second-string? I'm better than that!* Furious, she stormed out of the locker room.

When she arrived home, Lacy was watching TV. "How'd it go?" she asked, knowing that today was the day Shannon would have found out if she had been chosen for first-string or not.

"Don't ask."

"You didn't get it?" Lacy cried out and then regained her composure. "Well, don't let it get you down. It's only basketball. It's not the end of the world, you know?"

Shannon didn't say anything but went to her room to get ready for her date with Max. As the evening wore on, Shannon's foul mood persisted. Finally losing patience, Max said, "Shannon, will you let it go? It's just a game. In case you've forgotten, you're out with me. We're supposed to be having fun."

Over the next week, things didn't improve. Shannon continued to sulk. She considered quitting the team, tried to think of a way to sabotage Debra, and even get revenge on Coach Yancy. She couldn't believe this was happening to her. During practice, Shannon spent most of her time practicing on the sidelines while Coach Yancy worked with Debra on plays. She felt like a second-class citizen at school. People who used to pal around with her didn't say anything directly, but Shannon could tell they were talking about her getting passed over for the center position.

Even Max seemed to avoid her. He no longer waited for her before school or sat with her at lunch. Finally, on Friday he came clean. "Look, Shannon, I don't think this is going to work. I think we should see other people."

TRUTH UNPLUGGED:

A humble heart focuses on things that matter most and causes your steps to be sure.

"Why?" she asked in disbelief.

"I just want to be free to see other people my senior year," he responded with a shrug.

Shannon didn't buy it. She and Max had already planned their senior year. Together, they were supposed to be the homecoming king and queen. They had even talked about the prom and the senior trip. They had reveled in the fact that they were going to be the most popular couple during their senior year.

Later that night after the first football game of the season, she saw Max talking to Jana Stuart, the head cheerleader, and knew the truth. Max wanted to be part of a popular couple and she was no longer in the running. Second-string center didn't cut it.

Coming home after the game, Shannon found Lacy on the living room floor surrounded by bits of paper, scissors, glue, and markers.

"Hey, how was your night?" Lacy asked.

"Well, Max and I broke up, if that gives you any idea," Shannon admitted, beaten. Her perfect senior year was not turning out the way she'd planned.

"Well, thank God! My prayers have been answered. I don't think I could have handled a year of 'Rocky' hanging around," Lacy teased. "Now, you can live down here with the rest of us mere mortals. I have my sister back!"

With that, she threw Shannon a homemade card that said: You'll Always Be First-String to Me. Shannon laughed and grabbed her sister, tickling her until she was breathless.

"Tell the truth," Lacy said when Shannon had finally let her go. "Aren't you relieved you can play basketball for fun? There's no pressure to carry the team. You'll still get great scores and a scholarship offer, but most of the pressure will be on Debra."

Shannon thought about what Lacy had said. Although she wasn't entirely convinced things were better, she had to admit Lacy had a point. Maybe her senior year wasn't going to be such a disaster after all.

TRUTH LINK:

Dear Lord, I want to stay humble no matter what goes right or wrong in my life. I don't want to get caught up in superficial things, and I really don't want to base my self-worth or my value of others on temporary things such as looks, things, or position. Help me to keep pride out of my life. Amen.

POWER UP:

Pride is a dangerous thing. It sets you up for a fall without any warning. One minute you think you've got it all together, and the next minute you're flat on your back, wondering what happened. Worse than that, pride alienates you from people who care about you. When you finally fall, you're alone. Don't think your value, or others' value, comes from accomplishments, looks, or superficial things. God values each of us because of who we are to Him, and He wants us to value each other for the same reason. When we recognize that our value comes from Him, pride will no longer have a hold on us.

REFLECTION

Materialism

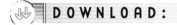

DOWNLOAD:

A life devoted to things is a dead life, a stump; a God-shaped life is a flourishing tree. Proverbs 11:28 The Message

Sydney stared at her reflection in the boutique mirror for several minutes. It was perfect! This was it, a three-quarter length, strappy, red designer dress that would make her junior prom a dream. She would feel like a starlet walking down the red carpet at the Oscars.

"Are you sure you want that dress, Sydney?" her mother asked, biting her lower lip.

"Yes, Mom. Don't you think it's amazing?" she responded.

"It's beautiful, honey, but I don't know that it's worth the price," her mother responded. "I think you look just as pretty in the other one."

The designer dress was way over Sydney's parents' budget. In fact, it was double what they'd said they could pay. They had told her that they would give her a certain amount of money for a dress, but anything above that would be her responsibility. So for the last two months, Sydney had done everything from raiding the money she'd saved to go to equestrian camp to working odd jobs after school. She just *had* to have this dress.

She knew her mother meant well by trying to get her to save her money, but she felt her mother didn't understand. Her parents loved her no matter what. She could be dressed in her old riding habit, smelling like sweat, her horse, and the barns, and they would think she was the most beautiful sixteen-year-old alive.

But Sydney's parents weren't taking her to the prom. Brad was, and Sydney wanted him to think she was the most beautiful girl there.

Three months ago, Brad Walters had asked her out on a date. Then two months ago, he'd asked her to the prom. They'd been dating ever since. Sydney still wanted to pinch herself. She couldn't believe that someone as cute and nice as Brad had asked her out. She really liked him. They had so many things in common: a love for horses and family barbeques and deep convictions about their faith. Sydney was convinced that this would be the best prom ever.

Three weeks later, Sydney was ready. She and her best friend spent the whole day preparing. Sydney's parents had paid for her to have her hair, makeup, and nails done at a salon. Now, looking at the final results, she felt completely put together. Her hair and nails were perfect, her makeup flawless, and her dress, shoes, and accessories—stunning. All she needed was to have Brad arrive.

Within minutes, the doorbell rang. Sydney's heart raced, hoping that he would think she was the most beautiful girl he'd ever seen.

As she walked into the living room, Brad turned and beamed. "You look fantastic!"

For the next hour, Brad and Sydney posed for pictures at her house and then returned to his house to pose for his parents too.

Normally, Sydney would have hated all the attention, but that night she floated through the air. She loved hearing everyone gush about how beautiful she and Brad looked together. It made all the money she had spent worth every penny.

For dinner, Sydney and Brad joined a few of their friends at The Trophy Club, a beautiful restaurant that overlooked a manicured golf course complete with an indoor waterfall and huge stone fireplace. Sydney thought her prom date was going even better than she had planned.

Just before dessert arrived, two of the guys began flicking a paper football across the table at each other. Everyone laughed at their antics. As they paused from their game, the waiter placed desserts in front of each person. As he turned to leave the table, someone wildly flicked the football. Without thinking, another reached to grab it out of the air right in front of Sydney, spilling her soft drink. She jumped, knocking her cheesecake off the table and into her lap. Shooting up from the table, Sydney watched in horror as the cheesecake slid down her lap onto the floor. Unable to think or say anything, she raced to the restroom.

Bursting through the restroom door, she began to sob. Her perfect night was ruined before it had really begun. She hadn't even made it to the prom yet. *How can I go now?* she wailed inwardly. For the next several minutes, Sydney tried desperately to get the stain out of her dress with a wet paper towel, but the harder she tried, the worse it looked. Now, instead of a dark smeary blob down the front of her dress, she also had flecks of white paper sticking to it. *This is the worse night of my life!* she thought.

TRUTH UNPLUGGED:

Material things don't determine your value.

Tap, tap, tap. Sydney heard a light knock on the bathroom door.

"Sydney, are you okay?" Brad called.

Sydney didn't know what to do. She wanted to disappear. Now, in addition to her ruined dress, her face was red and puffy from crying and her makeup was either streaked or washed away. Unable to think of an escape, she opened the door.

"Hey, Brad," she murmured. "Can you take me home?"

"You don't want to go to the prom?" he asked in earnest.

She frowned. "I can't show up looking like this. My dress is ruined."

Brad looked down at her dress and then back to her face. "I still think you look great," he said gently. "I wouldn't care what you wore. I just want to go with you. I still think we'd have a good time."

Sydney looked at him, puzzled. "Brad, I look awful. My dress is ruined. My makeup's streaked. I can't believe this happened." Sydney felt tears threaten to start again.

"Sydney, the guys are really sorry. If you want to go home, I'll take you, but I really meant it when I said I didn't care what you wore. I just like being with you. You could even wear my jacket so that people wouldn't see the stain. Or if you want to go home, we could go watch a movie and pop popcorn."

Sydney didn't know what to say. Brad really didn't care what her dress looked like. He just wanted to be with her. She looked down at her dress. The irony almost made her want to laugh. She had spent so much time worrying about her dress and working to pay for it, and now it was ruined. And what was worse—or maybe better—Brad didn't even care what she was wearing. He just liked being with her.

"Okay," she said. "Give me a minute to fix my makeup as best I can and then we'll go to the prom. But I *will* wear your jacket."

As bad as the night had begun, Sydney ended up having a blast. She and Brad laughed the whole night. In fact, she probably had a better time since she no longer had to worry about her dress.

For their prom picture, the photographer had them stand in a funny pose so that the stain on Sydney's dress wasn't visible. Those waiting in the picture line rolled with laughter watching them. For years to come, that picture reminded Sydney how little material things, such as dresses, jewelry, and makeup, really mattered. She kept it pasted to her bedroom mirror so that whenever she began to think her clothes determined her value, she remembered the prom and Brad, the guy who just wanted to be with her, no matter how she dressed.

TRUTH LINK:

Dear Lord, thank You for reminding me that things don't determine my value. You love me for who I am in You, and You've placed people in my life who love me for who You've made me. Please help me to remember that. Keep me from falling into the trap of thinking that I have to look a certain way or have certain things to be valuable. Amen.

POWER UP:

The news, Hollywood, magazines, friends, even family all tell you how to look, how to dress, and what to own. If you're not careful, you can begin to believe that these things dictate the kind of person you are. You can begin to think that if you don't have the perfect clothes, just the right car, or the ideal house, then you're no one. But that's not true. God is interested in who you are as a person, not in the material things around you. It isn't wrong to have nice things, but it is wrong to define yourself by them. The next time you think you need to have some THING to make you worthwhile, remember that one day, not too far in the future, that THING will be replaced by something newer. The true value God has put in you—love, joy, peace, kindness, etc.—will last forever.

THE CHALLENGE

Mentoring

DOWNLOAD:

Pass on what you heard from me . . . to reliable leaders who are competent to teach others. 2 Timothy 2:2 THE MESSAGE

Shawnda stood at the edge of the field, watching the first-graders pass the soccer ball back and forth, kicking it out of bounds and having to pull it from under bushes. They were possibly the worst team Shawnda had ever witnessed.

She couldn't believe her dad had forced her to volunteer to coach this little community team. According to her dad, she needed to "take some responsibility and realize that the world didn't revolve around her."

Give me a break, Shawnda thought.

The truth was, this was punishment for some of Shawnda's latest escapades. Last week, she'd taken her father's car without permission. She'd only gone over to a friend's house, but her dad hadn't been amused. And then there was the little miscommunication she'd had with her parents a couple of weeks ago. She'd told them she was going to a friend's house. Instead, she and her friends had gone to a party across town—and stayed out all night. By the time Shawnda returned home, her father was panicked and furious. He had spent the night driving all over the city looking for her. He had called the police and all of Shawnda's friends. It hadn't been pretty.

So in return for those incidents, Shawnda's dad had decided that she had too much free time on her hands. She needed something to do. After a few phone calls, her father had offered her help to coach an inner-city soccer team. Shawnda had played soccer for years in independent leagues. Over the years, she had played all the positions, gone to several soccer camps, and practiced for hours. She knew the game.

In addition to playing soccer, she was also a good student. If she stayed on her present course, she could possibly get a college scholarship. Her dad doubted that would happen if she didn't curb her other extracurricular activities. So to ensure that she stayed on the straight and narrow, she was now coaching for this pathetic little co-ed team four nights a week.

"Hey, you the coach?" a little girl asked, eyeing Shawnda.

"Yup. That's me. Coach Shawnda," she responded with more than a little sarcasm.

"You don't look like much," the girl said. "Do you even *know* how to play soccer?"

"Trust me, I know how to play," Shawnda said defensively. *Who does this chick think she is anyway?* she thought. *I can charge, dribble, pass, and juggle circles around these twerps.*

"We'll see," the little girl muttered as she walked off toward the other players.

That afternoon Shawnda gathered her new team for introductions. She counted twelve kids, ages 8-9, including Elizabeth, the one she had already met. All were dressed in old clothes and even older equipment. Though they were really young, Shawnda knew some of these kids were quite a bit older in life experience and hardship. They were tough—tougher than Shawnda had been at their age—quite possibly tougher than she was at that moment.

Following introductions, Shawnda had the kids take the field for practice drills. After watching them for a few minutes, Shawnda realized she needed to start with the basics—how to kick, pass, and even explain the rules of the game. *Boy, they need work,* she thought.

By the end of practice, everyone was exhausted, especially Shawnda. She wasn't used to having twelve kids demand her attention. They continually asked questions and distracted each other. What should have taken thirty minutes to explain and practice took an hour. Watching them wander home, Shawnda wondered if she could handle this.

"So are you gonna be here tomorrow, or are you gonna ditch us?" Elizabeth asked skeptically.

"I'll be here," Shawnda said weakly as she turned to face Elizabeth, wondering how this girl could read her so well. "What makes you think I won't?"

"You just don't look like somebody who wants to be here, like you're being forced to do this."

Inwardly, Shawnda was shocked that Elizabeth could see through her so easily. Taking up the challenge, she responded, "I'll be here."

Over the next few weeks, Shawnda worked hour after hour with the team. Although they weren't professional material, they did improve. By the end of their second game, their record was 1-1. Not bad for a team that hadn't won any games the previous season.

What surprised Shawnda more than anything was how much she enjoyed getting to know the boys and girls. At first, they'd barely spoken to her about anything other than soccer, but as the weeks went on, they'd come to her with a variety of questions— everything from faith and family issues to school and love. More and more Shawnda heard herself saying the same things to them that her parents said to her. She talked to them about responsibility and sportsmanship. She corrected them when they cursed or put each other down. She became more than just a soccer coach; she became a surrogate big sister.

Following one of the games, Elizabeth approached her. "Hey, Coach, you got a minute?"

Shawnda waited to hear what Elizabeth had to say. Of all the kids, Elizabeth had been the hardest to get to know. Slowly, she had started to trust Shawnda, but the progress had been very, very slow. Elizabeth lived with her grandmother and her three younger brothers and sisters. As the oldest, she carried the burden of taking care of her younger siblings while her grandmother worked.

"Coach, I got a question for you," she said hesitantly. "I gotta do a paper at school about the person I admire the most. And, well, I thought about it, and that's you."

TRUTH UNPLUGGED:

Look for opportunities to be an example, a mentor, of Christ's love, goodness, and wisdom to others.

Shawnda didn't know what to say. Touched and embarrassed, she said, "Elizabeth, that's really cool. I'm honored, but what about doing it on your grandma?"

"It has to be someone other than family," Elizabeth responded quietly. "I gotta ask you some questions about the qualities I admire and how someone like me can develop them," Elizabeth continued.

"Sure, I'll answer your questions. Why don't we get together after practice on Monday? We'll go to Cold Stone for an ice cream cone, my treat," Shawnda offered.

"Okay," Elizabeth said with a glimmer in her eye. "I like ice cream."

Following Monday's practice, Shawnda and Elizabeth enjoyed double-scoop ice cream cones while Elizabeth asked Shawnda questions. She asked why Shawnda became a coach, which Shawnda answered honestly. She asked what she enjoyed about coaching and why she continued to do it.

After thinking about it for a few minutes, Shawnda responded, "I like you kids. You have a lot of potential, not just at soccer, but as kids. I like being a part of watching you grow."

Elizabeth listened and slowly asked, "You think I got potential?"

Shawnda laughed, "Elizabeth, you have more potential than anyone I've ever met before. I really mean that."

Elizabeth beamed as she finished her ice cream.

Later, at home, Shawnda thought about her time with Elizabeth and the rest of the kids. She couldn't believe that only a few weeks ago she had thought teaching them was a punishment. Now, it was a bright spot in her day. She loved the idea that what she said and did with these kids mattered. Who'd have thought that she could be someone they would look up to and one day want to be like.

She thought back to the first day when Elizabeth had asked her if she would continue to be their coach. Shawnda had taken her question as a challenge, and she was so glad she had.

TRUTH LINK:

Dear Lord, I want to pass on the same love, goodness, and wisdom to others that You've shown to me. Help me to see opportunities where I can give to others by instructing and encouraging them. Help me to be a mentor for You. Amen.

POWER UP:

Can you think of people who have taught you how to act or think? A parent? A coach? An older brother or sister? A teacher? Maybe they didn't even say anything directly, but you learned just by watching them. You may think mentoring is reserved for older people, but it's not. If you consider how much you pass on to your younger brothers, sisters, or friends, you will realize that mentoring is something you do every day. It's powerful. It means showing someone else the love of Jesus through your actions and your words. It's about helping them become the person God desires them to be.

A CROSS IN THE ROAD

Stealing

DOWNLOAD:

"Don't steal. Don't lie. Don't deceive anyone."

Leviticus 19:11 THE MESSAGE

"Lighten up, Marianne! You act like I killed somebody," Leah said, rolling her eyes, as they drove home from shopping at the mall.

"Leah, you *stole* that wallet, and I was with you. Not only is it wrong, but if you had been caught, they would have thought I was in on it with you," Marianne challenged.

Leah had said before that she sometimes took things from stores, but Marianne had never taken her seriously. This was the first time that she had done it when Marianne was around . . . and then gloated about it afterwards.

"Look, I'm sorry if it makes you uncomfortable. I just saw it and took it. No big deal. I won't do it around you anymore," Leah said.

Leah dropped Marianne off at her house. As Marianne walked in the front door, her mother called from the kitchen saying that dinner was ready. Marianne dropped her bags at the door and joined her family for dinner. As she passed her dad's famous barbequed chicken to her sister Milly, her mother asked, "Are you okay, Marianne? You look upset about something."

Marianne shrugged. "I had a bad day." She had never been one to hide her emotions—especially from her parents. Marianne was convinced they had internal radars because they always knew when something was wrong.

As the family chatted about their day, Marianne couldn't stop thinking about Leah's shoplifting. She tried to tell herself that whatever Leah did didn't affect her, but she couldn't help feeling that it did. She and Leah did everything together. They'd been best friends for years and this was the first time that Marianne had ever been ashamed to know her.

After dinner, she went into the living room where her father watched the news. On the TV was a story of a professional shoplifting ring that had been busted.

"Dad, why do people steal?" Marianne asked, watching the story unfold.

"Some people do it for money. Some for the thrill," he said simply.

"Does stealing make somebody a bad person? I mean, if somebody stole something small once or twice, does it mean they're a thief?" Her dad turned and quietly looked at her for a moment.

"I don't like to think anyone is beyond help, but if they steal, they *are* a thief. It doesn't matter how big or small the thing is that they stole. They can change and decide not to do it again, but if they're caught—even if they did it only once or twice— they'll still pay the consequences," he said.

"What happens to them?" Marianne asked.

"They could go to jail or get probation. Even if they don't serve time, it can still be a mark on their record. It'll come up whenever they try to get a job or apply for college. It's a big deal," he said. Then pausing a moment, he asked, "Why do you ask? You seem pretty interested for it to only be a casual question."

Marianne gulped. She didn't know how to respond without betraying Leah. "Well, it's just come up lately. I know somebody who's taken some stuff, and I just wondered," she responded.

Her dad exhaled slowly and nodded. "What do you think you should do?"

"I don't know. We're friends, but I don't want to be around when they do it."

"You think you'll be guilty by association?" he asked.

"Yeah, that and, well, it's just wrong. It's something I wouldn't do and I hate the fact that they think it's fun. It's not like they even need the stuff. They just see something and take it," Marianne responded.

"Well, I'd love to tell you what to do, but I think you already know. So instead, I'm going to pray that you have the courage and clarity to handle this, but if you need help, I'm here."

TRUTH UNPLUGGED:

Stealing is not a game. It can affect you for the rest of your life.

"Thanks, Dad."

Over the next few weeks, Marianne continued to ponder Leah's shoplifting. She tried to put it out of her mind, or ignore it, but she couldn't. Every time she and Leah got together, she couldn't help wondering if Leah was shoplifting. She thought back to gifts that Leah had given her out of the blue and questioned whether or not they'd been stolen.

She found herself refusing to go places with Leah. If Leah needed to stop by any store, Marianne made some excuse to go home first. If Leah wanted to get a soda at a gas station, Marianne stayed in the car. She just didn't want to be near Leah if she took something.

After school one Friday, Leah asked Marianne to go to the mall for the end-of-the season clearance sales. Marianne couldn't because she was going out to dinner with her family, not that she regretted declining to go. Just the thought of going shopping at the mall with Leah made her nervous.

The following day, Leah came over with a new blouse for Marianne. "Where'd you get this?" Marianne asked.

"I went shopping yesterday and saw it. I knew it'd look great with the new capris you got a few weeks ago," Leah responded, smiling. "Don't you just love it?"

"Did you pay for it?" Marianne asked. She hadn't meant to be so blunt. The question had just popped out of her mouth.

Leah looked disgusted. "What's that supposed to mean? This is what I get for giving you a gift—some superiority complex? Can you just get over yourself for a minute?" Leah replied hotly.

"You didn't answer my question," Marianne said, "so I guess you didn't pay for it." Shaking her head, she handed the blouse back to Leah. "I can't take this."

Fuming, Leah snatched the blouse from Marianne and stormed out the door.

Marianne felt like she'd been punched in the stomach. Leah was her best friend, but there was this chasm between them that couldn't be crossed, at least not until Leah stopped stealing. Marianne had tried to convince herself that she could avoid being involved in that part of Leah's life, but she realized she couldn't. Every time they were together, it stood between them. Marianne didn't trust her enough to go shopping or do anything with her anymore. And what was worse was that Leah continued to do it although she knew Marianne disapproved. It made Marianne wonder how strong their friendship was if Leah wouldn't stop shoplifting to save it.

For the rest of the weekend, Marianne thought about what she needed to do. She talked to her dad again, and they prayed together.

On Monday, she found Leah after school. "I need to talk to you." She could tell Leah was still angry. "You are my best friend and I love you, but I can't be a part of this." Her eyes filled with tears. "It's against what I believe. I've tried to convince myself that I could just avoid that part of your life, but I can't. It hurts me to say it, but I don't trust you anymore. Whenever we'd go to a store or you'd give me a present, I'd wonder if you've stolen it. So until you quit stealing, we can't hang out together."

Leah looked at her angrily. "If that's what you want, fine. I don't need a best friend who's so self-righteous anyway," she said and stalked away.

Marianne watched her best friend leave as tears rolled down her face. She'd never thought that there would be a time when she and Leah wouldn't be friends. Her only consolation was that even though Leah may not consider *her* a friend, she would always consider Leah one. She just recognized that they couldn't hang out together. They'd reached a place where their beliefs differed, and it wasn't something they could ignore.

Lord, please help her to see the truth, Marianne began to pray as she started for home, *and help me to get through this.*

TRUTH LINK:

Dear Lord, I know what Your Word says about stealing, and I don't want to be a part of it. Help me not to be tempted to steal or to hang around others who do. Help me to live honestly for You and to choose friends who do the same. Amen.

POWER UP:

Some people think stealing or shoplifting is a thrill, a kind of game, but it isn't. It's playing with fire. If you are caught, you'll face legal consequences—some for the rest of your life. Even if you're not caught, at best, you'll still become someone who can't be trusted. At worst, stealing will become an uncontrollable habit. Make the decision to stay away from stealing and people who steal. If stealing has already become a habit that you can't break, pray for God to give you the courage to get help from a parent or a pastor. You are not alone; Jesus is always waiting to help you.

NOT THE END OF THE WORLD

Peace

DOWNLOAD:

"Peace I leave with you; my peace I give you. I do not give to you as the world gives. Do not let your hearts be troubled and do not be afraid." John 14:27 NIV

Maria stared down at her returned chemistry test. She couldn't believe it—a D. She'd studied for days. Her throat constricted and the room spun. *What will this do to my grade?* she wondered in horror.

In all her years, she'd never received a D, not even on a homework assignment or pop quiz. She was an A student who could become the valedictorian her senior year. Unlike many of her peers, she took her schoolwork seriously. She never blew it off. If anything, she went overboard. Last year, her algebra teacher had urged her to "relax and enjoy school," but she couldn't.

Her parents had high hopes for her and often said, "Maria, you can do anything you set your mind to, but you have to study. You won't get anywhere without a good education." Her parents weren't wealthy by any means, but what they did have they generously gave to her. They would do anything to ensure that she received the best education possible, and Maria knew it. She felt responsible to give school her all—nothing less than 110 percent.

That's why she spent her afternoons and weekends poring over her books and notes. Any extracurricular activities she participated in had to look good on a college application. In fact, she spent most of her free time thinking of ways to improve her standing. While many students fulfilled their college class requirements and then took frivolous classes, Maria wouldn't even dream of it. She filled her schedule with the hardest classes, and then pushed herself to pull an A every time.

"Are you okay, Maria?" her friend Juanita asked. "You look pale."

Speechless, Maria showed Juanita her paper.

"Oh, no!" Juanita gasped. "Maria, I'm so sorry. What happened?"

Unable to talk for fear she would cry, Maria shrugged.

"Why don't you talk to Mr. Hernandez after class? Maybe there's been some mistake," she offered.

After class, Maria approached Mr. Hernandez' desk feeling defeated. "Mr. Hernandez, can I talk to you a minute?" she squeaked out.

"Maria, I thought you might want to meet with me. I suppose you're shocked by the grade you received. Honestly, I was a bit surprised too. Did you not understand the material?"

Maria struggled to keep her composure, "I thought I did. I don't know what happened." Then, placing her test on his desk, she continued, "Can you tell me what I did wrong?"

"Well, look here," he said turning the test over, "you answered the first part of the essay question on quantum numbers and some of the second part, but you didn't answer the third part. That question was 50 percent of the grade."

Maria looked at the test again. Mr. Hernandez was right. She'd overlooked half of the question. She must have gotten into a hurry and missed it. "What does this mean for my overall grade?" she asked.

"Let's see. You had an A going into this test. Now, you're average is a high C. With the next test, you could still bring it up to a high B," he said.

Maria couldn't believe it. She'd never received anything less than an A. "So there's no way I can make an A now?" she asked, her voice shaking.

Mr. Hernandez looked compassionately at her. "I don't think it's likely. You may get close, but I doubt it."

Crushed, Maria quickly left Mr. Hernandez' room and rushed to the restroom. She cried so hard she could barely breathe. *How can I tell my parents? How could I let this happen?* she wailed inwardly. Unable to compose herself, Maria missed her next class. Instead, she called her mother to come get her from school. When her mother finally arrived, Maria jumped into the car. Though Maria hadn't told her mother what had happened, Maria had conveyed that something was terribly wrong.

"Honey, what has you so upset? I've never seen you like this before," her mother asked, concerned. Maria struggled to answer but couldn't stop crying long enough to formulate the words. Instead, she pulled the test out of her bag and handed it to her mother. After looking at it a moment, her mother responded, "Oh, honey." Then pulling Maria into a hug she comforted her, "It's okay. Everything is going to be okay. Did you talk to your teacher? Do I need to talk to him?"

Catching her breath for the first time, Maria responded, "No, I already talked to him. I messed up on the essay question." Then feeling the tears sting her eyes again, she confessed the worst part, "Mom, he said I can only make a B in the class now."

"It's okay. We'll talk to your dad and work everything out. And if you get a B, then that'll be okay. It's not the end of the world," her mother comforted.

Later that evening, after Maria's father came home, he and her mother talked in hushed tones in the kitchen while they prepared dinner. Then at dinner, her father asked, "How are you doing? Your mother told me what happened with your test and your grade."

Maria nodded, pushing her food around on her plate. "I'm sorry, Dad. I messed up on the essay question. I knew the answer, but I forgot to finish it."

"Well, I'm sorry about your grade. It's a shame because I know you could earn an A, but really, I'm more concerned about you. You seem to be taking this so hard and I'm worried that we've pushed you too much," he said, looking to her mother for affirmation. Maria didn't know how to respond. She'd always been an A student. It's what she'd always been and she knew it was what her parents expected. To her, there was never an option other than getting an A.

TRUTH UNPLUGGED:

God's peace can help you walk through any situation.

"Your mother and I have talked about it and we *want* you to do your best. That makes us proud. But if your best is a B, that's okay too. We don't want you to expect perfection from yourself every time. Everyone makes mistakes. You just have to learn from them and move on," he said.

Maria listened to her father, but she didn't understand exactly what he was talking about. She was an A student. She didn't get Bs. She couldn't just switch gears and start believing Bs were okay.

After dinner, she and her parents gathered in the living room for family devotions. During their devotions, they read from the Bible and then prayed. It was something they tried to do every night. It was Maria's turn to read from Matthew 26. In the chapter, Jesus warned Peter that he would deny Him three times before the rooster crowed. Peter said it would never happen, but at the end of the chapter it said that he did.

When Maria finished reading, she believed she kind of understood Peter's distress. He'd made a mistake that he regretted deeply. Though Maria didn't compare her mistake on her chemistry exam to Peter's denial, she did understand how difficult it was to live with mistakes. But then she also remembered that Peter had gone on to be used by God; his mistake wasn't the end of the story for Peter.

As she prayed that night, Maria asked God to give her wisdom about what had happened and help her not to make the same mistake again. But she also asked Him for peace as she walked out the rest of this grading period, knowing that she couldn't redeem her grade. She had to live with her mistake. Truthfully, it might cost her the valedictorian position, something she had worked years to achieve, but she knew with God's help she would be okay.

As the days passed, she understood what her father had meant at dinner that night. Sometimes, all she could do was her best. Everything else, she just had to let go.

TRUTH LINK:

Dear Lord, please show me how to have Your peace in my life. When I face difficult situations—even ones that are my fault—I pray that You'll help me to deal with them in peace. I don't want to live in turmoil over things I can't change, and I need Your help to accomplish that. Amen.

POWER UP:

Everyone faces challenges—disappointments, mistakes, or expectations that are difficult to live up to. Even when those challenges come, you can still have peace in your life. You don't have to let worry, anger, or fear overtake you. Instead, you can pray for peace to be with you and remind yourself that Jesus hasn't left you to deal with things on your own. Through prayer and studying your Bible to see how others faced similar challenges, you can find the answers you need. And if you need someone to give you face-to-face advice, ask God to show you whom you should speak to—a parent, a counselor, a pastor, or some other adult. Remember: you are **NOT** alone. Jesus is there to help you find answers and give you peace as you work through even the most overwhelming situation.

FACE THE TRUTH

Forgiveness

DOWNLOAD:

Be even-tempered, content with second place, quick to forgive an offense. Forgive as quickly and completely as the Master forgave you. Colossians 3:13 THE MESSAGE

Beth saw Camille sitting with a group of friends at the far corner of the cafeteria. Nervous, she walked their way. She wondered what Camille would say to her. Up until last week, they'd been best friends. Everyone knew them as the daring duo—always thinking up crazy, funny things to do. Usually they conspired on harmless pranks. That is, until last week.

Last Wednesday, someone had vandalized Coach Dawson's office, rifling through it and toilet papering everything in sight. Nothing had been broken, but everything—chairs, tables, pictures, and more—had been turned upside down with confetti and silly string covering it.

Of course Coach Dawson was an easy target. Ask any student, and they would tell you that the coach was in a perpetual bad mood. The day of the incident, he had forced one class to run laps for an entire class period because one student had talked back to him. By the end of the laps, students were close to passing out on the hot field. Unfortunately, Beth had been the student who had talked back to him. She'd meant her comment as a joke, but Coach Dawson had been in an especially bad mood. After class, Beth had received angry comments from several students in class. She'd been on everyone's hit list.

So when Camille's school jacket had been found in Coach Dawson's office, no one doubted that Camille had committed the offense. Everyone knew Camille and Beth were tight. They assumed that Camille had meant to vindicate Beth by getting back at Coach Dawson.

Camille had denied the incident, but unfortunately that only made her appear to be guiltier. Coach Dawson and the principal had called her parents, suspended her for two days, enrolled her in detention for two weeks, and forced her parents to pay for the damage. According to Coach Dawson and the principal, she'd gotten off easy. This sort of violation could have been turned over to the police and become a permanent mark on her record, affecting her college admissions.

As Beth approached the lunch table, the group slid down to make room for her. They were in the middle of discussing the incident and Camille's punishment.

"Wow, I can't believe you're able to come back to school. Remember Jenny Werner last year? She vandalized the art room and they kicked her out of school for good," one friend said.

"They wanted to kick me out, but my dad talked them out of it by promising to pay for all the damage and having me do community service here at the school for the rest of the year," Camille responded dejectedly.

"So who do you think did it? Everyone knew Coach Dawson ticked everyone off by making them run all during class," another stated.

Camille looked around the group, her gaze falling on Beth, "I can't say who did it. All I know is that it wasn't me." Beth remained quiet during the discussion. Then, unable to stand Camille's scrutiny, she excused herself from the table.

After school, Beth braced herself as Camille approached her in the parking lot. "Why didn't you say something? I know you were the one who toilet papered the coach's office because you had borrowed my jacket earlier in the day."

Beth shifted uneasily. "I'm sorry, Camille. I didn't mean for you to get into trouble. I left your jacket by accident. I was just angry that Coach Dawson made us run during the whole class period. Everybody was mad at me, and I just wanted to get back at him."

Camille scowled, "So why didn't you come forward when you knew they'd accused me?"

"Can you imagine what my parents would have done to me if they'd found out? They'd have freaked—probably even sent me to boarding school or something," Beth desperately explained.

"Yeah, they probably would have said the same things that mine did. Do you realize that I am on restriction for the rest of the school year? And this summer my parents are making me work for free for them just to pay them back? So basically, this stunt of yours has cost me the next six months of my life." Not waiting for an answer, Camille stormed off.

Beth felt sick. Everything had gotten way out of hand. She'd only meant to play a joke on Coach Dawson. She hadn't meant for Camille to take the fall, but what could she do? If she spoke up now, everyone would hate her for not saying something sooner. And she was certain her parents would ground her for eternity.

For several weeks following the incident, Beth didn't see Camille much. She was either in class, in detention, or picking up trash around the school. After Camille's detention ended, Beth began staying after school to help Camille pick up the trash. She tried desperately to make it up to her friend. Although Camille thanked her for the help, they didn't speak much as they worked.

During lunch, their gang of friends continued to sit together. Beth wanted everything to go back to the way it had been before the vandalism. It took quite a while, but slowly things seemed to get back to normal.

One day after school, Beth approached Camille. "Hey, Camille, do you want to go grab a burger? I'm starving."

Camille looked away. "I wish I could, but I can't. See ya."

TRUTH UNPLUGGED:

Forgiveness sets you free from whatever or whomever caused the hurt.

As Camille started to walk away, Beth stopped her, "Are you gonna hold this against me forever? I said I was sorry."

Camille looked right at her. "Look, I forgive you, but I'm still on restriction. I can't hang out after school."

"Will you be able to hang out this summer? Maybe come swim and lie by the pool at my house?" Beth asked.

Before she left, Camille promised to ask her dad. She was set to work all summer, but maybe her dad would start easing up on the restrictions.

As Beth watched Camille leave, she felt sick. Camille had forgiven her even when she hadn't deserved it. As she headed for home, she felt ashamed. Camille was a better friend to Beth than Beth was to Camille. It was something Beth decided to change.

I need to talk to Mom and Dad when I get home, Beth thought. Then she made plans to confess and face the punishment for vandalizing Coach Dawson's office, something she should have done months ago.

TRUTH LINK:

Dear Lord, please help me forgive those who have hurt or offended me. I realize I need to forgive them, but I need Your help. I need to know how to forgive them once and for all, and I also need to know how to handle myself around them in the future. Amen.

POWER UP:

Have you had a difficult time forgiving someone who has hurt or offended you? You may think: **BUT YOU DON'T KNOW WHAT THEY DID. THEY DON'T DESERVE TO BE FORGIVEN.** And you're right. They don't **DESERVE** forgiveness, but forgiveness isn't for them, it's for you. As you forgive, you free yourself from the pain and bitterness. You become free to care for others instead of living in fear of being hurt again or held captive by that sickening feeling that hits you whenever you see the offending person. It may take time, but make the decision to forgive and continue to make that decision whenever painful memories come to mind. In time, the memories won't be painful. At that point, you'll know you're free. And what a great feeling it is!

THE BEST BIRTHDAY PRESENT EVER

Love

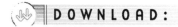 **DOWNLOAD:**

Be devoted to one another in brotherly love. Honor one another above yourselves. Romans 12:10 NIV

"I know what I want for my birthday," Shannon proclaimed. Her golden curls danced around her 8-year-old head.

"Oh, yeah? What?" Stephanie asked as they walked out the front door for school.

Stephanie dropped Shannon off at school each morning on her way to the high school. Shannon had admitted to feeling so cool by having her big sister drop her off instead of her parents. Stephanie didn't mind. She loved Shannon and found her amusing. Shannon was by far her biggest fan.

"I wanna go to the Tween Jam concert next month," Shannon announced. "It'd be my first concert."

Cautiously, Stephanie asked, "Who do you want to take with you?"

"You, silly. It'll be so cool for us to go together," she said emphatically. "We'll have a blast! We can get matching T-shirts and everything!"

Stephanie smiled nervously. There was no way she could be seen at a Tween Jam concert. The Tween Jam concert tour catered to kids under the age of twelve. Stephanie was sure she would die from embarrassment if anyone found out she'd gone, let alone saw her there. Oh, no, it wasn't going to happen.

"Shannon, maybe you should think of something else for your birthday," she ventured.

Shannon gazed at her with deep brown eyes. "Why?" she asked innocently.

"I just think you could come up with something even cooler," Stephanie offered.

After a few minutes of silence, Shannon turned to Stephanie. "I've thought about it and I wanna go to the Tween Jam concert with you," she said, nodding her head in excitement. "You said I could pick *anything* under $30 and this *would* be. And I think we'd have the *coolest* time ever."

Unable to think of a quick response, Stephanie remained quiet. *O Lord, get me outta this. It'll be so embarrassing,* she thought.

Over the next month, Stephanie tried to subtly convince Shannon to pick another birthday present. She did *not* want to be the only teenager at the concert surrounded by five hundred screaming, little pop princess wannabes. But no matter what she said, she couldn't dissuade her. Shannon said over and over again that they would be the coolest kids at the concert.

For the week prior to the big event, Shannon came to the dinner table each night gushing about her plans. The best Stephanie could do was convince Shannon not to make matching T-shirts, but rather to find things in their closets that somewhat matched. Thrilled by her willingness to dress alike, Shannon scrounged through their closets to come up with outfits—glitter, spangles, and all.

On the night of the concert, Stephanie looked at her reflection in horror—a red shirt with white stars on it, gaudy rhinestone earrings, and a sequin-covered baseball cap. *Could this get any worse?* she wondered. Then she saw Shannon, dressed in a similar outrageous outfit. It looked like Stephanie had cloned herself at half the size. *I can't do this,* she told herself. *I thought I could, but there's no way I'm going out in public looking like this.*

As she turned to tell Shannon that she was going to change clothes, her little sister squealed, "We look *so* beautiful! I'm gonna get the camera so Mom can take our picture." And away she ran.

On the way to the concert, Shannon jabbered non-stop. She'd proudly told all her friends and her friends' friends and her friends' parents and her friends' brothers and sisters that *she* was going to the Tween Jam concert with her big sister. Stephanie groaned inwardly, *Now everyone knows.*

TRUTH UNPLUGGED:

Show the love of God by putting others first.

Inside the arena, they found their seats: 4th row, dead center. To make matters worse, the three rows in front of them and the seats around them were mostly empty. So there was no hiding in the crowd. Stephanie felt like she was on display.

As each band played, Shannon jumped, clapped, screamed, and danced until she was glistening with sweat. "Come on, Stephanie," she urged, trying to pull Stephanie to her feet. "Stand up with me."

Stephanie nervously looked around. Other than parents, she was the only person over twelve in the place. "No, Shannon, I just want to watch."

During intermission, Stephanie had no choice but to take Shannon to get autographs and refreshments. As they stood in line, Shannon stood quietly.

"Hey," Stephanie nudged, "aren't you having fun?"

"Yeah, I just wish you were more fun to be with. I thought it would be so cool to come with you, but you're just sitting there. You're not dancing or clapping or anything."

"Sorry. This is just kind of a little kid thing," Stephanie said.

"But it's *my* birthday present," Shannon pleaded, looking up at Stephanie.

Stephanie felt ashamed. She suddenly saw the event through her sister's eyes. She saw how important the concert was to her. She realized how cool it was for her little sister—her biggest fan— to go to her first concert with her big sister. She'd allowed what others might think of her to keep her from giving her little sister a great birthday. Shannon deserved better than that.

"I'm sorry, Shannon. I should have gotten more into the spirit of things. I'll tell you what. Why don't we make the rest of the night the best ever?"

"How?" Shannon asked.

Looking around, Stephanie came up with a plan. "To start with, you stay here and get the autographs for this band, and I'll go over there so I can get the autographs for that band. That way we'll get both before the second half of the concert starts."

"You mean it?" Shannon asked, wide-eyed.

"Of course. Just don't talk to anyone, and as soon as you finish, stand at the end of the signing table until I get there. Don't move, okay?"

Shannon agreed, and Stephanie was off, getting into the spirit of things.

For the rest of the night, they sang, screamed, clapped, and jumped up and down until they were exhausted. Stephanie had to admit she had had a good time once she'd forgotten to notice everyone else and focused on her little sister.

On the way home, Shannon and Stephanie sang all the songs again at the top of their lungs. Shannon bounced in her seat and proclaimed the night was "the best of my whole life."

Stephanie laughed, "Ya know, I think it's right up there for me too." She knew she'd never forget taking her little sister to her first concert and giving her the best birthday present ever.

TRUTH LINK:

Dear Lord, I want to be someone who shows love and kindness to others. Please show me how to put others first every day so that I can be an example of Your love. Amen.

POWER UP:

It's hard to continually put others first. It can be very uncomfortable, but as you do, you communicate a lot. You show that other person how valuable they are, and you become an ambassador of God's love to them . . . and the world.

FIRST IMPRESSIONS

Judging Others

If you refuse to act kindly, you can hardly expect to be treated kindly. Kind mercy wins over harsh judgment every time.

James 2:13 THE MESSAGE

Cherise walked into the youth hall and quickly scanned the group. This was her first time to come and she wasn't excited about it. Unfortunately, her mother had insisted. As the new kid in town, she dreaded meeting people for the first time. She still felt irritated and off balance.

After growing up in her hometown with friends and family surrounding her, her mother had decided to take a job in a new city. "We need a fresh start," she proclaimed. Cherise disagreed. The two years since her parents' divorce and her father's subsequent relocation to another state had left Cherise feeling very alone. She felt that the only thing that kept her sane were her grandparents, her Aunt Kay, and her old church friends. Now, they were three hours away and Cherise felt more alone.

The new town didn't look much different from the old one, except for the people. It had similar supermarkets, malls, arcades, and parks, but it still felt foreign. Cherise didn't know anyone except her mom and brother. Later in the summer, she'd start school at a strange, new high school. She dreaded that too.

From across the room, a girl about Cherise's age, dressed in the latest, expensive fashions, approached her with a big smile, "Hey, there! You're new, right?"

Cherise returned a tight smile and thought, *What? Is she kidding?* In two seconds, she sized this girl up—rich and ditsy with the perfect life. *We have nothing in common,* she concluded.

"My name's Monica. And I'm *so* glad you're here!" she said a little too enthusiastically.

Cherise introduced herself and allowed Monica to take her around and introduce her to the other kids. Most of them were nice enough, but Monica bugged her.

"Oh, you *have* to come sit by me. I'll fill you in on all the youth group's summer activities. You just *have* to come to *all* of them," she rattled on. Cherise felt she'd entered the twilight zone and been adopted by this over-the-top, Banana Republic-wearing guardian angel.

No, thank you, she thought.

Throughout the rest of the service and even afterwards, Cherise desperately wanted to get away from Monica. She tried to talk to the other kids around her, but Monica didn't take the hint. And even afterwards, when the group decided to go to a nearby ice cream parlor, Monica insisted that Cherise ride with her. By the end of the night, Cherise felt like she'd overdosed on Monica. The girl was bouncy and flashy to a fault. Cherise found her nauseating.

By the next week's service, Monica had already called Cherise three times. After trying to gently brush her aside, Cherise discovered Monica didn't understand subtlety. So she decided to be blatant. When she entered the youth group room, she made it a point to walk over to a group of girls on the opposite side of the room, away from Monica. And when Monica tried to get her attention, she ignored her. *Maybe she'll get the hint that I don't want to be her bosom buddy,* Cherise thought as she slid into a seat as far away from Monica as possible. Later, as she left the room, she found herself face-to-face with Monica. Monica gave her a weak, wounded smile and then quickly looked away. Satisfied that Monica wouldn't bother her anymore, Cherise left.

Three weeks later, before the service dismissed, the leader asked for prayer requests. A few raised their hands. Cherise noticed Monica carefully raised her hand.

"I'd like everyone to pray for my mom and me. We're really going through a hard time. Everybody knows that my parents divorced earlier this year, but they're still working out stuff like what will happen to our house. My dad wants to sell it, but if they do, my mom and I will have to move. It's not even like my dad needs money or anything. He's just angry and wants to get back at my mom, even though he's the one who left us. Anyway, I really don't want to move and go to a new school," Monica said sadly.

Stunned, Cherise bowed her head along with everyone else to pray for all the requests. She'd had no idea that Monica had those kinds of problems in her life. From the outside, she always looked so carefree and put together. Now Cherise realized how much they had in common—their parents' divorce, losing a home, and moving.

Cherise realized that Monica had really never done anything to her other than try to make her feel welcome. In return, Cherise had jumped to the conclusion that they could never be friends and had brushed her off. She felt sick inside realizing that she'd never given Monica a chance to become a friend—a friend perhaps God had intended for her to have all along.

After the service, several people were going out on a burger run. Cherise crossed the room and asked, "Hey, Monica, do you want to go get a burger with us?"

Monica looked at her in confusion. "Okay," she said cautiously.

"Good, you can ride with me, if you want."

"Sure. That sounds good," Monica responded. Then hesitating, she asked, "Um, Cherise, why do you want to hang out with me now? I got the feeling you didn't like me."

Embarrassed, Cherise fidgeted. "I judged you and shouldn't have. I was wrong. Without first getting to know you I thought we had nothing in common. I'd like another chance to get to know you."

Monica thought about it a second and then smiled. "Okay," she said simply.

As the group gathered at Burger King, Cherise listened—really listened—to Monica as she interacted with the group. She couldn't believe that she'd missed so much. Monica was probably

TRUTH UNPLUGGED:

Don't judge people harshly. Instead, treat them with the same mercy, compassion, and kindness that you want to receive.

one of the most sincere people she'd ever met. And not only sincere, but funny too. What Cherise had taken as "ditsiness" was just a bubbly personality. As the group continued to talk and joke back and forth, Cherise realized that she finally didn't feel alone anymore. *Maybe moving to this town wasn't such a bad idea*, she thought. *Just look at all the cool people I've met.*

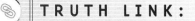
TRUTH LINK:

Dear Lord, forgive me for passing harsh judgment on people. Instead, help me to see them through Your eyes—with mercy, compassion, and kindness. Remind me to treat everyone the same—regardless of what I think they deserve. In that same way, I pray that You'll bring people to me who will treat me with mercy, compassion, and kindness.

POWER UP:

It is easy to fall into judgment. You see someone who looks or acts differently than you and you instantly either feel a connection, "We could be friends," or repulsion, "We have nothing in common." It's easy to do, but unfortunately, when you judge someone harshly, you risk the opportunity to have a great friendship. Eventually, you will be treated with the same harsh judgment. People will begin to recognize you as someone who classifies people as "good" or "bad," "worthy" or "unworthy." When you are in need of a little mercy, kindness, and compassion, instead of receiving the benefit of the doubt, you very likely won't find it. It's a vicious cycle that's better to avoid. Instead of trying to classify someone, be open to the friendships God wants to bring your way. Allow yourself to celebrate the differences in people. Along the way, you'll be pleasantly surprised to find at least one unexpected friend.

THE DOUBLE LIFE

Church

DOWNLOAD:

Let us not give up meeting together, as some are in the habit of doing, but let us encourage one another. Hebrews 10:25 NIV

"Hey, Deanna, it's Erin. You want me to come get you for youth group?"

"No thanks, I'm skipping tonight. I'm going over to Kirsten's," Deanna explained.

Silence.

"That makes the third week you've missed youth group, and you haven't made it to church for the last two Sundays either. What's up?" Erin asked with concern.

"Nothing. I just don't feel like going to youth group or church," Deanna said flatly. She'd attended church all of her life, but since her mom started working on Sundays, she didn't feel like she had to go.

"Sounds to me like you're starting a bad habit," Erin countered. "You know Kirsten isn't the kind of person you need to take cues from. Don't get me wrong. She's fun, but she parties and runs with a pretty wild crowd."

Deanna expected this from Erin. Erin was at church every time the doors were open. Though Deanna and she used to hang out together a lot, Deanna had decided that church wasn't as necessary as she'd once thought. "You're just judging her. You don't even really know her. Besides, we're not partying. We're just hanging out at her house and watching a movie."

Again silence.

"Say what you will. I'm still praying for you," Erin said simply.

Just as Deanna thought, Erin would turn this into some super-spiritual lecture. *Why can't she just leave me alone,* Deanna thought as she said her good-byes and hung up the phone. She and Erin were friends, but Erin needed to lighten up. *Just because I don't want to go to church doesn't mean I'm not a Christian.*

Later that evening at Kirsten's, Deanna and she discussed her decision to blow off youth group.

"You couldn't pay me to go to church," Kirsten said with disgust. "What a bunch of holy rollers!"

"It's not so bad," Deanna said, feeling a bit uneasy as Kirsten laughed at her. She wasn't used to having to defend her faith or her friends from church.

The next day, Erin called Deanna again. "Hey, we missed you last night. Lots of people asked about you. You know, there's a lock-in planned for next Friday night during spring break? We're gonna have the whole church to ourselves with pizza and games and movies all night long. You should come."

Deanna promised to think about it. She wasn't sure what she wanted to do. She was having so much fun hanging out with Kirsten and her other new friends that she couldn't imagine giving up a Friday night to hang around at a church party.

When she mentioned it to Kirsten later, Kirsten laughed again. "Are you seriously considering going?" she asked in shock.

"Deanna, if you haven't figured it out yet, lemme help you out: church is for losers. You don't want to go running around in some lame church all night, do you?"

Deanna felt torn. On one hand she had Erin trying to get her to go back to church, and on the other hand she had Kirsten telling her she'd be a loser if she did. She didn't *hate* church. She just wanted to take a break from it for a while. She'd been going almost every week of her life because her mom forced her to go. Now, she had to make up her own mind. She knew that, according to everything she'd been taught, Kirsten wasn't the best friend to have. But on the other hand, she was fun.

On Thursday of spring break week, Deanna and Kirsten were hanging out with a few other new friends when Kirsten handed Deanna a glass. "Here, try this."

"What is it?" Deanna asked uneasily.

TRUTH UNPLUGGED:

Don't think of attending church as an obligation. Instead, consider it an opportunity to grow in who you are in Christ and meet others who share your faith.

"Just a little pick-me-up. Trust me, you'll like it," Kirsten laughed.

Deanna took a sip. The liquid burned the back of her throat and continued to burn all the way down. She coughed and sputtered. She felt like her insides were on fire. Everyone laughed.

"Told you you'd like it," Kirsten nodded. "I took it from my parents' cabinet. Go on, have some more."

Though Deanna hadn't wanted to drink the alcohol, she didn't want the others to think she couldn't take it. So all evening she drank with the rest of them. She didn't return home until the early morning hours. Since her mom had to be at work early the next morning, Deanna stumbled her way through the dark, quiet house and finally collapsed onto her bed.

As soon as she lay down, she felt the room spin. Nausea hit her. She knew she was going to vomit. Rushing to her bathroom, she made it just in time. But with each hurl, she felt another one coming. Wave after wave hit her like a cement wall.

In the morning, she woke up on the bathroom floor to the sound of someone banging on the front door. Still feeling lousy, she opened the door. Erin stood there, giving her a strange look.

"What happened to you?" she asked with concern.

"Nothing. I just woke up," she responded. Just then, she felt another wave of nausea hit her, and she ran. Erin followed her to the bathroom.

"Are you okay?" she asked. Then, as if a lightbulb flashed on, she said, "You've been drinking."

Coming up for air, Deanna scowled. "So what. Don't get all high and mighty on me."

Erin shook her head. "Yeah, I can see I'm the one with the problem here." Then going to the linen closet, she grabbed a washcloth and soaked it with cool water. "Here, put this on your forehead."

Taking a seat on the edge of the tub, Erin watched her friend. "Deanna, what are you doing? You are so much smarter than this."

"I just wanted to have some fun with my friends."

"Your friends, huh? If they're so great, why'd they get you drunk? And where are they now?"

"Don't preach at me. I really don't need it," Deanna said weakly. Her head throbbed.

"Don't you get it? I care about you. I don't want you heading down this road." Then shaking her head she added, "I just came over here to see how you were doing. That's all."

Over the next several hours, Deanna slowly started feeling better. She slept, ate, and finally felt well enough to lie on the couch and watch TV. Erin stayed with her the entire time, just to make sure she was okay. Later that afternoon, as Erin started to leave for the lock-in, she asked Deanna one more time to come.

Deanna thought about it. She figured it was the least she could do since Erin had spent the entire day taking care of her—not to mention that the pizza sounded really good.

When she walked in the door at church, her old friends from youth group gave a shout, welcoming her back. As the evening wore on and the group played flashlight chase, had shaving cream fights, stuffed themselves with pizza, and watched movies, Deanna couldn't remember why she'd stayed away so long. She had a blast! It was as if she'd never left, and it was sure more fun than drinking and getting sick with Kirsten and her friends.

Deanna thought back to when Kirsten had called her church friends losers. After the last 24 hours, Deanna could promise that her church friends weren't losers. They just didn't have to drink at a party in order to have a good time, and that sounded pretty smart to her.

TRUTH LINK:

Dear Lord, thank You for showing me where to go to church. I know I need to be a part of a church body. I pray that You'll show me just where I need to go and help me to meet good friends. Amen.

POWER UP:

There comes a time in every person's life when he or she has to decide whether they will attend church. When you're young, your parents may take you, but as you get older, you choose. Don't think of church as an obligation; think of it as an opportunity to meet with great people who believe the same way you do. You'll find real friends who want what's best for you, not people who are trying to drag you down. Some don't have parents who encourage them to go to church. They're on their own. If that's you, take time to pray about where you should go. Pray that you'll find the right church with the right friends. Then allow Jesus to lead you to your church home. Soon you'll find a place of refuge where you can learn about God and enjoy the people there.

DEFENDING HER TERRITORY

Jealousy

DOWNLOAD:

Where jealousy and selfish ambition exist, there is disorder and every evil thing. But the wisdom from above is first pure, then peaceable, gentle, reasonable, full of mercy and good fruits, unwavering, without hypocrisy. And the seed whose fruit is righteousness is sown in peace by those who make peace.

James 3:16-18 NASB

"Go, Jacob!" Abby cheered as loud as she could for Jacob as he raced down the soccer field, heading for the goal—his third for the day.

Abby and Jacob had been next-door neighbors and best friends for years. They'd grown up together. As toddlers, their mothers had let them play together in their playpens. In elementary school, they had played soccer after school, and during the summers, they had raced to the public pool where they had endlessly challenged each other in the game Marco Polo. Nowadays, they spent hours discussing the Bible and doing homework together. People often teased them about being girlfriend and boyfriend, but they'd always just blown it off. They were just friends, more like brother and sister really.

As the soccer game ended, Abby ran over to Jacob to congratulate him on winning a tough game. They gave each other a high five as the rest of his teammates jumped up and down. "Way to go," Abby said excitedly. "You scored three goals. That's amazing!"

"Thanks! Did you see that last one? That guy almost tripped me but I caught myself and kept going. But, boy, for a second, I thought I was going to eat it," he said, smiling a victorious smile.

"Yeah, I did. Hey, do you want to change and then go get a burger on our way home?"

Jacob's smile faltered. "Oh, I'm going to get something to eat with Tracy Guiness," Jacob said.

Abby's smile disappeared. "Oh, okay. I'll see you later then." Abby and Jacob had always eaten lunch together after his games, so Abby was confused. Tracy was a new girl at school, and Jacob had a couple of classes with her. He'd mentioned her a few times, but Abby had never imagined they liked each other.

For the next few days, Abby couldn't get rid of the nagging feeling that their friendship was changing. She noticed he was hanging out with Tracy in between classes and after school. Abby tried to take it in stride, but she felt deserted. It wasn't that she disliked Tracy. In reality, she didn't even know her. But right now, it didn't matter. Tracy was the enemy.

The following week, Abby arrived early at youth group. She hadn't seen Jacob in several days and hoped to catch up with him before the group began. Jacob didn't arrive until about five minutes before the group began, and Tracy was with him. Abby couldn't believe he had brought *her*. Youth group was one of the activities Abby and Jacob had enjoyed the most together. *How could he bring her?* she questioned.

Jacob waved to her and motioned for Abby to join them, but Abby looked away, taking a lone seat at the back of the group.

After the group dismissed, several teenagers gathered for refreshments and Abby joined them. From behind her she heard, "Hey there, why didn't you come join us? I wanted to introduce you to Tracy."

Abby glanced his way and then turned away. "I didn't think there was room," she said coolly. "Besides, I already know who Tracy is. You don't have to introduce us." Abby knew she was being snotty, but she couldn't help it. She didn't *want* Tracy to be there.

Jacob frowned, looking confused. Abby knew he was trying to figure out what was bothering her. *Let him figure it out,* she thought.

"Well, do you want to go with us to get ice cream on the way home? A few others are going to join us too," he said.

"Nah," Abby responded. "I don't want to crash your date."

"It's not a date," Jacob said shortly. "I told you other people are coming too."

"Good for you," Abby said sarcastically, "but I'm not interested." Then turning, she gathered her purse and Bible and left. She knew Jacob watched her leave.

Out in the parking lot, Abby climbed into her mother's car. Tears came to her eyes. She felt she was on the verge of losing her best friend. She didn't want things to change. Now she had to share him with Tracy or any other girl he chose to date. As tears flowed down her cheeks, she looked up as the group headed to the ice cream parlor. Several people, Jacob and Tracy included, laughed on their way to their cars. Abby watched them, feeling left out. She wanted to be part of the group, but unable to swallow her pride, she drove home.

Later that night, as she sat on her bed studying, her phone rang. Answering it, she heard Jacob say. "What was up with you tonight? Why'd you blow me off like that? And why don't you like Tracy? What'd she ever do to you?" Jacob's questions came like rapid bullets from a machine gun.

"I just didn't feel like entertaining," Abby said weakly.

"Yeah, well, I couldn't enjoy myself all night. My best friend blows me off and doesn't want to hang out with the girl I like. How's that supposed to make me feel?"

Abby's emotions ranged from contrition to anger. On one hand, she felt bad about ruining Jacob's evening, but on the other, she wanted him to hurt like she was hurting.

When she didn't say anything, he continued, "Oh, I get it; you're jealous. I have another friend who's a girl and you can't stand it. That's why you've been mean to Tracy even though she never did anything to you. I thought you were bigger than that."

Abby adamantly denied it, but inside she knew he was right. She'd been jealously defending her turf, her position in Jacob's life. And the more she defended it, the further she pushed him away, and the worse she felt.

TRUTH UNPLUGGED:

Don't allow jealousy to poison your relationships and drive a wedge between you and your friends. Trust God and your friends to keep your best interests at heart.

After they hung up, Abby thought for quite a while about the situation. Was she ready to lose her friendship with Jacob just because he had started dating someone? He was the best friend she'd ever had, but unless she came to terms with it, she would lose him. She took a few minutes to pray. She asked Jesus for forgiveness for her pettiness and jealousy, and then prayed He would show her what to do. Then she came up with a game plan. First, she'd apologize to Jacob. Then she'd see if he would introduce her to Tracy. Maybe she'd see about getting to know some other friends so that all her time wouldn't be spent waiting for Jacob. Somewhat satisfied with her plan, she turned off the light to go to sleep. She knew her plan wasn't foolproof, but it was a start. And right now, she needed a place to start.

TRUTH LINK:

Dear Lord, please forgive me for becoming jealous and allowing strife to enter my friendship. I need Your help to know how to deal with what I'm feeling. Show me if my friendship is just changing or if I'm overreacting. Either way, help me to be secure in my relationships, act with integrity, and rely on You in everything I do. Amen.

POWER UP:

Jealousy is a dangerous element in friendship. It can end even the best of relationships. Before you know it, you begin to view every comment, look, and action with suspicion. Then strife enters the picture, and the relationship is one step closer to death. Instead of giving in to jealousy, ask God to show you how you can become more secure in your friendships. It's not ever easy to lose a friend, but friendships do change. At one point, you may mean the world to each other, and then circumstances can change and you find yourself hanging out with different people. It can be a difficult transition, but don't succumb to jealousy and strife. Whether the change is real or imagined, you must trust God to bring the right relationships into your life at the right time. He wants what's best for you all the time—even in your friendships.

SCARS

Inner Healing from Abuse

🔽 **DOWNLOAD:**

He heals the heartbroken and bandages their wounds.

Psalm 147:3 THE MESSAGE

Tamara unpacked the rolls of toilet paper and stacked them neatly on the shelf. She carefully pulled the old inventory to the front and placed the newest arrivals in the back. It was Tuesday night, a perfect time for restocking because there were never very many customers. Tamara scanned the bar codes to record them into the inventory system. It wasn't a difficult task, but it had several necessary steps that helped keep the inventory system straight.

Tamara had held her job in the drugstore for about six months. After her mother and stepfather had divorced, Tamara and her mom needed the money. Tamara didn't mind. It was a break from her home. Things were better now that her stepdad had left, but her home still held too many memories—painful memories that Tamara desperately wanted to forget.

"Tamara, don't forget to rearrange the bandage and adhesive shelves," Mr. Jefferson reminded her. "I'll be in my office working on some paperwork."

It was a big deal for Mr. Jefferson to leave her alone with the customers and money. It had taken awhile for her to earn his trust. She remembered when she'd first come to apply for the job; she could barely look him in the eye. She'd felt worthless and very distrustful of men in general, but he'd hired her anyway. Over time, she came to trust him and realized that he wasn't like her stepdad. He was kind and respectful. He wouldn't use or hurt her.

After Tamara finished restocking the toilet paper, she moved to the bandage aisle. She pulled boxes of newly received inventory closer to the shelves and began to unpack and fill the holes. The bell on the front door rang, announcing a new customer. As customary, Tamara stopped what she was doing and greeted him.

The older man returned her greeting with a smile and walked toward her. "I'm looking for a special ointment," he said as he handed her a piece of paper listing the ointment's long pharmaceutical name. "I can't pronounce it, but it's supposed to be great for healing burns." Tamara knew of the ointment and led him to the shelf where it was stocked. As she showed him the different sizes available, she noticed the shiny, pink, slightly mangled skin on the side of his neck. Seeing that she'd noticed his burn, he explained. "I was in a warehouse fire about six months ago. They didn't think I'd make it. I had a mask on my face so I didn't get burned there, but it got the rest of me pretty good—my neck, chest, and back." Turning, he showed her his left ear. "See that," he said, pointing to the lower part of his ear. "They reconstructed most of it." Tamara hadn't noticed the difference before, but now she saw that his left ear was different—lumpy and slightly askew from his right.

Tamara had never met a burn survivor. She asked, "Does it still hurt?" Then embarrassed at what must have been a stupid question, she looked away.

The man laughed. "Don't be embarrassed; that's a good question. You know, it sure did hurt at the time, but it doesn't anymore. I can remember days when the pain was so intense, I wanted to die just to make it stop, but now the only pain is in my memory. So when I remember the pain—either because of a nightmare or just sometimes when I think about it too much, I look at the scars. They remind me that the pain is behind me and the scars can't hurt me."

After the man purchased his ointment and left, Tamara returned to restocking the bandages. She continued to think about what the man had said: "The scars can't hurt me." The comment went around and around in her mind. She thought of how this man had been hurt, spent months recovering, and now had scars that would remain for the rest of his life. Tamara thought, *But his scars are on the outside; mine are on the inside.*

TRUTH UNPLUGGED:

Painful memories don't have to control you. You can live without the pain of the past or fear that it will happen again.

She thought about the Christian counselor her mother had insisted she see after her stepfather had left. He'd encouraged her to pray for God to heal her memory and help her to trust people—especially men—again. She'd done that. She'd prayed. Though she hadn't had any lightening bolts come from the sky, she had met several nice men over the last several months—the counselor, her boss, Mr. Jefferson, and now, even this man with the burns. Through them, she'd found kindness, trust, and understanding. It was true, she still had her painful memories, but they were scars now—slightly discolored, mangled memories that lived in the past. And as the burned man had said, "The scars can't hurt me."

TRUTH LINK:

Dear Lord, You know all my painful memories. I realize that they'll always be with me, but I ask for Your healing. I pray that You will help me to see them as scars that don't hurt anymore and don't affect my future. I pray that I'll be able to see them as a part of my past that no longer hurts me. And I pray that You'll help me to see the beautiful things You've placed in my life. Please let me realize how much You love me and are working in my life. Amen.

POWER UP:

Do you have a painful memory—a hurt or abuse—that you think you'll never be able to get over? Maybe you've tried to get past it, but you feel trapped by the recollections. Painful experiences can leave you angry, hurting, distrustful of people, and feeling unlovable, but that's not what God wants for you or believes about you. He wants you to be free from the pain of the memories, and He wants you to accept His love for you. That doesn't mean you won't remember the event, but it means that it won't have power over you anymore. If you are unsure how to accept Jesus' love and you need a person to talk to, ask God to show you someone you can talk to who can help you deal with the memories—perhaps your parents or a counselor. They won't judge you or condemn you; they will only want to help you.

SOMEONE WHO UNDERSTANDS

Loneliness

DOWNLOAD:

By yourself you're unprotected. With a friend you can face the worst. Can you round up a third? A three-stranded rope isn't easily snapped. Ecclesiastes 4:12 THE MESSAGE

Alisa walked across the lit stage, paused, twirled, paused again, and then returned to her spot with the other finalists. Her hair was perfectly coiffed, her gown was exquisitely tailored, and her smile dazzled. It was the Miss Mistletoe pageant and she felt ridiculous.

Her mother had been a model and beauty queen in her youth, and she had high hopes for Alisa to follow her lead. Most of Alisa's life had been spent like other kids—playing and attending school, with a few ballet classes and music lessons sprinkled in for good measure. Alisa hadn't minded. In fact, she had enjoyed all of it. But after her fifteenth birthday last spring, her mother decided it was time for her to shine. By shining, she meant becoming the next Miss America. So here she was, twirling on stage, answering questions about her future hopes and dreams—

things about which she really didn't have a clue—and desperately trying not to trip in her three-inch stilettos.

"Trust me. It's for your own good," her mother had assured her. "One day you'll thank me."

Alisa knew her mother meant well. She just wanted to give Alisa every opportunity in life, but Alisa simply didn't want to be a model or Miss America. She'd rather be attending slumber parties and football games with friends. Now, her weekends were spent either struggling to keep up with her schoolwork or attending competitions. The friends she used to have either drifted away or no longer wanted her around. Several had assumed her new life was so glamorous that she must "think she's too good for us," which was never the case. In fact, she'd have given anything for a friend.

Lord, I feel so alone. I'm trying to keep my mother happy, but right now I just need someone to talk to and have fun with. Someone who won't think I'm a prima donna because I'm in beauty pageants.

After the competition ended, Alisa returned backstage to pack her stuff. She'd made it to the final ten, but no further. She wasn't disappointed; she was still a new kid on the pageant block. She congratulated the winner and said hello to a few contestants. She'd tried to get to know a few people, but it was hard since they saw each other only at competitions, and when she competed, she had to keep her mind in the game. That didn't mean you couldn't be nice, but there wasn't enough time to get to know people very well.

As she packed her curling iron and rearranged her makeup bag, one of the other contestants walked over to her. "Hey, I heard your answer to that last question. You did really well."

Alisa stopped and smiled. Though she'd recognized the girl from other competitions, she'd never talked to her. "Thanks, it's nice of you to say so."

"My name's Angela, by the way. I've seen you at other competitions. You're good."

"Thanks, I've seen you also. You're good too. I really liked your evening dress," Alisa said.

"Thanks. Um, don't you live in Stevensville?" When Alisa confirmed that she did, Angela continued, "I live only about 30 minutes away in Fairfield. Maybe we can get together sometime and go to the mall or sneak an ice cream cone?"

Alisa laughed. "Sure, that sounds like fun." They exchanged phone numbers and promised to call each other the next week.

When Angela did call, Alisa discovered they had a lot in common. They both took voice lessons from the same teacher, both loved to shop, and thought Baskin Robbins' peanut butter and chocolate ice cream was the premier flavor in the 31 flavor lineup. They also shared a profound faith in God.

> ## TRUTH UNPLUGGED:
>
> If you are lonely and need a friend, ask God to send you one. He cares about every aspect of your life—even your friendships.

Over the next few weeks, they called each other several times and finally found a time to meet at the mall. They had a fun time trying on different outfits, some of them hilariously ugly. They laughed and talked their way through half the shops before ordering lunch in the food court.

"You know," Angela confided as she ate, "I prayed that God would send me a friend." She shifted a little uncomfortably before continuing. "I know that probably sounds crazy, but it's been really hard to keep friends since I started competing. They either don't understand or get tired of me never being available to do anything."

Alisa smiled. "I know exactly what you mean. I prayed for a friend too." They fell quiet for a minute. Alisa thought of how lonely she'd been and how God had answered her prayer for a friend. As excited as she was to have a new friend, she was even more excited to know God had heard her prayer.

TRUTH LINK:

Dear Lord, I am really lonely and I would love to have a close friend to talk with. Please send me a friend—someone who shares my interests and my faith in You. Amen.

POWER UP:

Do you wish you had a good friend with whom you could talk and laugh? Maybe you're the new kid in town and you don't know anyone. Or perhaps you've recently become a Christian and you and your old friends don't have as much in common anymore. Or maybe you've just never had a close friend you could count on. If so, ask God to bring someone into your life. Don't think that talking to God about your loneliness or your desire for a close friend is too trivial. It's not. He cares about the things that concern you—even friends.

THE PROOF OF LIFE

Prayer

DOWNLOAD:

Believing-prayer will heal you, and Jesus will put you on your feet. And if you've sinned, you'll be forgiven—healed inside and out. James 5:15 The Message

Beep. Beep. Beep.

The hospital machines around Isabel's grandfather beeped and whirled. The sound was somewhat comforting, considering that their silence would have announced the end for him. The buzzing also helped to fill the void of not knowing what to say. Isabel felt helpless as she watched him drift in and out of consciousness.

"Come on, Grandpa. Sit up and talk to me," she pleaded.

"Keep talking to him," one of the nurses had encouraged when she came in to change one of his intravenous bags. "He may be able to hear you."

So Isabel had. She'd told him about her day at school, her friends, her boyfriend. But after awhile, she didn't know what else to say other than, "Please don't leave me, Grandpa."

It wasn't that she didn't have other family; she did. But no one—not her parents, brother, sister, grandmother, or anyone else—knew her like he did. She was convinced he'd taught her everything worth knowing about life. He'd taught her about courage, friendship, and love. She'd listened to everything he'd said—well, almost everything. The only thing she couldn't quite get her head around was his faith in God. She'd attended church with him, but to her, it was just pretty music and plenty of words. She understood people getting together as a community—he'd taught her about that too—but to believe in something she couldn't see every day, well, that was just too hard.

"Isabel, would you like to come with me to the chapel to pray for your grandfather?" her grandmother asked.

"No, Grandma, I'd like to be here when the doctor comes by," she responded.

"You know, honey, the doctors don't know everything," her grandmother responded gently.

Isabel looked at her for a second before turning back to her grandfather. "Grandma, the doctor is the only one who can help him now." Inside, she felt angry that her grandmother had given up on him. What did she mean that the doctor didn't know everything? He was the only one who could offer them any help.

Thirty minutes later, the doctor came in for his morning visit. Isabel and he exchanged greetings. After watching him review her grandfather's charts, she asked, "How is he?"

"A little better," he said, never lifting his eyes from the chart as he wrote. "The heart monitor shows an improvement in one of the areas that was unresponsive."

Isabel was encouraged. She had faith that whatever the doctor prescribed would work. She felt confident that the medicines would help bring her grandfather home soon.

When her grandmother returned, Isabel shared the good news. Her grandmother smiled knowingly, "Yes, that's what I prayed for."

Isabel didn't argue with her, but she believed the doctor had helped her grandfather, not God. God may be up there watching the events unfold, but Isabel didn't think He really cared. He was just a silent bystander.

Another day passed, and again her grandmother invited her to go pray in the chapel. Again, Isabel declined. She waited for the doctor to make his rounds. Again, there was slight improvement. Her grandfather had opened his eyes and spoken to her grandmother late the previous evening. The hospital staff felt confident that he was improving.

On the following day, after another positive report, Isabel stopped the doctor on his way out of the room. "Doctor, thank you for helping my grandfather. I know if it weren't for you, my grandfather wouldn't be improving," she said.

TRUTH UNPLUGGED:

God wants to hear from you, so take time to talk to Him each day.

The doctor smiled. "I wish I could take credit for his condition, but I can't. Just tell your grandmother to keep praying."

After he left, Isabel sat down beside her grandfather and held his hand. She didn't know what to think. Why would her grandmother's prayers make any difference? Surely the doctor didn't think that prayer had something to do with her grandfather's improvement. It must just be nature taking its course.

Later that evening, Isabel and her grandmother continued to sit beside her grandfather, talking to him and each other. As they laughed and remembered a time when Isabel's grandfather had taken her for Saturday morning donuts across their lake by motorboat, Isabel's grandfather opened his eyes. He smiled. "I love to hear the laughter of my best girls," he said weakly. They rushed to his side and bent over him, laughing and encouraging him to get better. Then focusing on his wife, he said, "I've felt your prayers, Alice."

Isabel's grandmother smiled, smoothing his hair back onto the pillow. "You didn't think I'd give you up without a fight, did you?"

He chuckled and then closed his tired eyes. "That's my girl," he said before falling asleep.

As Isabel silently watched her grandparents, tears came to her eyes. She'd known all her life that they followed God, but she never could understand it. She'd always wanted something tangible to hold on to—something more than just a church building with people and pretty music. Now, watching them, she knew she'd indeed received something tangible. Their faith was real. God had listened and answered her grandmother's prayers. Her grandfather's life was proof of that.

The next day, when her grandmother asked her to go to the chapel to pray, Isabel didn't hesitate. She knew she'd miss talking to the doctor, but it didn't matter. She finally understood she was talking to a higher source, one with more answers and more power that the doctor would ever have.

TRUTH LINK:

Dear Lord, sometimes I forget to consult You about life, but I want to change that. Help me to remember to pray and include You in every area of my life. Amen.

POWER UP:

Prayer is an important part of living your life in God. Sometimes you'll see immediate answers to your prayers, and other times it will take time. Regardless, continue to pray for God's presence in every situation and listen as He directs you. Look for His hand as He works things out. You may even want to keep a notebook of the things you pray about. Then, as they're answered, record them. Over time, you'll see how much God works on your behalf. He isn't some faraway being who watches your life with mild interest. He is a part of everything you do and He's working on your behalf.

THE SACRIFICE

Giving

 DOWNLOAD:

"Give away your life; you'll find life given back, but not merely given back—given back with bonus and blessing. Giving, not getting, is the way. Generosity begets generosity."

Luke 6:38 THE MESSAGE

"Diana, we need to have a family meeting," his father said seriously. "Go get your brother and meet your mother and me in the living room."

Family meetings were serious. It was the kind of meeting her dad had called when her parents had decided to move the family across country, when her mother had returned to work, and when her grandmother had died. Usually, it was a time when the entire family came together as a united front for a serious matter. Anything that needed to be said was said to everyone at the same time so that no one was left out. The meetings were usually life-changing and always put Diana on edge.

As the family sat down together—Diana, her mom, her dad, her brother, Ben, and her older sister, Meagan—Diana looked around for Meagan's husband, Chad. Meagan and Chad had married a little over two years ago. They lived across town, close to the university where Chad was in training to be a doctor and Meagan studied to be a teacher. Just when Diana was about to ask where Chad was, she took a closer look at Meagan. Her eyes were swollen and red from crying. *Oh, man, this has to be serious,* Diana thought, hoping that something terrible hadn't happened to Chad.

"We're here together to discuss a pretty serious matter," her father began. Then looking at Meagan, he asked, "Do you want to tell them?"

Meagan, who held tightly to her mother's hand, choked out, "Chad and I are getting a divorce."

Stunned, Diana looked from her dad to her mother and then back at Meagan. She was speechless.

"Chad and I have been having problems for a while now," Meagan continued. "Things have been really tight with money and school. On Monday, he told me he'd been seeing someone else and wants a divorce. Yesterday, he moved out." Diana watched as her parents consoled and hugged Meagan.

"What this means," her father began in a shaky, emotional voice, "is that Meagan is going to move home for a while. She can't afford her apartment all by herself. And a lawyer is going to be expensive, so we need to help her out. Diana, you're going to have to share with Meagan. We're all going to help her move this weekend, so any plans need to be canceled. Everyone needs to pitch in. Any questions?"

Diana couldn't think of any at the moment. She moved over to give her sister a hug. Her mind was blank. After consoling her family for a while, she went up to her room for a retreat. She needed to collect her thoughts. With one announcement, she'd lost a brother-in-law, gained a roommate again, and lost her weekend.

Slowly, the realization sunk in. It wasn't that she wasn't compassionate toward her sister, but she'd waited for years to have a room to herself. She finally had space for all her stuff—posters, a desk, her computer, a CD player, and more. In her room, no one told her to change the music. No one got into her stuff, and she didn't have to share space with an older, bossier sister. Feeling slightly overwhelmed, she turned on her music and pulled out her scrapbook supplies. For the next two hours, she lost herself in the music and added pages to her youth group's yearly memory book.

On Saturday, Diana's parents woke everyone up early to get a head start on the day. For two days, Diana had slowly moved her things to one side of the room. Since space was limited, about half of Diana's things had to go into storage. The important things—like her clothes, computer, and CD collection—stayed in the room, but other things moved into the attic.

"Can't we convert the attic or basement into another bedroom for Meagan?" Diana had pleaded as she packed her things. She'd wracked her brain trying to think of an alternative to losing her room, but her parents hadn't budged. Neither the attic nor the basement was set up for a bedroom, and converting either one was too expensive to consider right now.

The family piled into a car and a truck to go to Meagan's apartment. In the truck with her dad on the way over to Meagan's, Diana

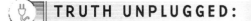

TRUTH UNPLUGGED:

As you give to others, you become God's hands to the world.

casually asked how long Meagan would live with them. "I'm not sure," her dad responded sadly. "I sure never saw this coming. It'll take awhile for Meagan to get on her feet again. She may not be able to move out until after she gets her degree next year."

"So I have to live with her for a year?" Diana asked in shock.

"Diana, trust me; this isn't easy for anyone. I know you're disappointed, but I really need you to give a little on this," her dad said, glancing over at her. "Your sister really needs our support right now." Diana didn't answer. Frustrated, she stared out the window.

Meagan's apartment was bare by the time Diana arrived. Half the furniture was missing, walls were blank, and cabinets were empty. Diana felt the hopelessness in the place. Not long ago, it had been a colorful newlywed apartment with lots of life and love, but now she felt the desperation. She walked through the small apartment, labeling and moving boxes to the door so Ben could load them onto the truck. In the bedroom, her sister sat on the stripped mattresses with her head in her hands, crying. Diana almost turned to leave, but then moved forward and sat beside her. She didn't know what to say, so she remained silent.

"Do you think God will forgive me?" Meagan whispered.

"For what?" Diana asked earnestly. "God knows Chad left, not you." Her protective nature rose to attention.

Meagan let out a cynical chuckle. "Yeah, he left all right. I feel like such a failure. Here I am, a twenty-one-year-old, soon-to-be divorcée who lives at home with her parents. Something is definitely wrong with that picture."

Looking at her distraught sister, Diana realized that losing her room was a minor thing. Putting her arm around Meagan, she gave her a quick hug. Feeling tears well up in her eyes, she tried to lighten the mood. "Well, I'll share my room, but the bathroom is another thing. I'm not waiting two hours each morning for you to get ready. There's a garden hose in the backyard. That's it. That's all you get," she teased. Hearing Meagan laugh, she knew she'd accomplished her goal.

Within a few hours, the apartment was empty and the family turned to leave. Watching Meagan take one last, sad look around the apartment, Diana knew at that moment that she'd have given her sister anything. She wasn't looking forward to a roommate again, but she realized her room was more than just a room for

Meagan. It was a refuge, a home she needed right now, and that was one thing Diana could give her.

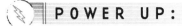

TRUTH LINK:

Dear Lord, please help me to have a giving heart. I want to remember that some things are bigger than I am, and that I don't always have to have my way. I know that sometimes I can't see past my own wants and needs, so please remind me to put others first. Amen.

POWER UP:

A giving heart is more than just giving your tithe or your offerings. Although those are very important, it is harder to give of yourself. It's hard to defer to someone else and put their needs first, but that's exactly what God asks us to do. As Christians, He wants us to be participants in caring for each other. You're important and what you give to others is important. So the next time you're asked or feel led to give of yourself for someone else, remember that God is using you. You are His hands and feet to others and that's a very important place to be.

THE PROM NIGHT DECISION

Sex

DOWNLOAD:

There's more to sex than mere skin on skin. Sex is as much spiritual mystery as physical fact. As written in Scripture, "The two become one." Since we want to become spiritually one with the Master, we must not pursue the kind of sex that avoids commitment and intimacy, leaving us more lonely than ever—the kind of sex that can never "become one."

1 Corinthians 6:16-17 THE MESSAGE

"So what are you and Leif doing after the prom?" Emily asked as Carly twirled in front of the mirror showing off the new, full-length prom dress she'd just bought.

Carly didn't answer right away. She continued to look at her reflection in the mirror. She'd been planning for her prom since her first day of high school. She'd known the kind of dress she wanted to wear—long and black with lots of sequins. The only thing that she hadn't known was who her date would be . . . until now.

Six months ago Leif Davies had moved to town, and shortly afterwards he had asked her out. She'd known he was a catch from the beginning. He was good-looking, athletic, and funny. Within just a few months of arriving, he'd become one of the most popular guys in school. All the girls were dying to go out with him, and much to Carly's delight, he'd asked her.

They'd been together ever since.

"I don't know. Leif's planning it," Carly said simply, unable to meet Emily's eyes. She wasn't sure she could tell Emily the truth. She and Leif planned to go to The Sterling, the nicest hotel in town, for a few hours.

Carly tried to treat it casually. She'd watched it on TV shows, studied it in classes, and heard people talk about having sex and losing one's virginity. *It's no big deal,* she kept telling herself. It was a natural part of life. And, of course, she loved Leif. She was ready.

Okay, so maybe Leif wouldn't be the guy she ended up marrying. She *was* only 17 years old and couldn't imagine getting married for years and years. But that was okay. No one really expected people to wait to sleep together until marriage, did they? In her mind, she remembered all the times she had heard about saving sex for marriage.

She tried to ignore the gnawing feeling inside that went all the way down into the bottom of her stomach. She loved Leif. She did. She loved him. He was wonderful, and sometimes when they were together, she really wanted to go all the way. Their time together was passionate. He was passionate. He made her feel things no other guy ever had.

So she had to be ready.

The weeks before the prom passed quickly. Since it was the end of the school year, Carly had lots to do—graduation to attend, finals to take, money to raise for church youth camp, and of course, finish preparations for the prom. She'd already made appointments to have her hair, nails, and makeup done. She'd purchased her shoes and ordered Leif's boutonnière. Now, all she had to do was buy accessories.

She kept thinking about the night that she and Leif were supposed to spend together. He had promised to take care of everything—make the reservations for the limo and the hotel, pack a romantic picnic basket, and buy condoms. They had talked about everything—well, almost everything. Some things were just a little too uncomfortable for Carly to discuss, but they'd covered the basics. They wanted to have sex, not a baby, so they had to take precautions.

Strangely, Carly noticed how often the subject of sex had come up before the prom, usually in the form of a warning. It was everywhere—at school her anatomy and physiology teacher talked about how sex was never completely safe, regardless of what birth control was used. Then, in church, the youth pastor talked about the spiritual significance of sex. Even her mother brought it up when one of her friend's daughters became pregnant. Usually sex wasn't a daily topic of conversation, but now it seemed that Carly couldn't get away from it.

The night before the prom, Carly laid out everything she needed for the next day. She was sure it would be the best night of her life. But why then did she have that gnawing feeling in her stomach again? *I'm ready for this. I'm ready,* she kept saying to herself over and over just as she had done for the last several weeks.

Sitting down on her bed, she thought about the last few weeks and how nervous and uneasy she'd felt. *What's my problem?* she wondered, grabbing her favorite childhood toy, a one-eyed stuffed bunny that had been rubbed bald by years of snuggling. *Lots of teenagers have sex. Why can't I? It's not like it's bad as long as you love the person, right?* Over and over in her mind, the questioned tumbled. She kept hearing her youth pastor talk about the joy of saving sex for marriage. *I'll never know that,* she thought. *I guess I'll never know the joy of loving only one person and having only one person love me,* she thought with a touch of sadness.

Shaking her head, she threw her bunny aside and stood up with determination. *This isn't the dark ages; people don't wait for marriage anymore. So what if I won't be a virgin on my wedding night?*

After a day of primping and preparing, Carly was ready. Her dress was perfect. Her hair had turned out exactly as she'd imagined. She loved her makeup, and her nails looked great too. She was ready.

As she came out of her bedroom, her mother gasped. "Honey, you look beautiful!"

"Thanks, Mom," Carly beamed. "I hope Leif thinks so too."

Her mom watched her for a moment and gave her a wistful smile. "I'm sure he will. Not that it really matters as long as you know it. God thinks you're beautiful and His is the most important opinion." Carly smiled in response as her mother started snapping her picture.

A few minutes later, Leif arrived. After having a few pictures taken together, Carly and Leif started to leave. "I'll be praying for you to have a great, safe night," her mother whispered as she hugged her one last time.

Strange, Carly thought as she and Leif walked down the front walkway to the limousine. *Why did Mom seem so serious? Does she know?*

TRUTH UNPLUGGED:

God isn't punishing you by asking you to save sex for marriage. He is protecting you from the hurt that can come from sex outside of a marriage relationship.

The prom was surreal. Twinkle lights, decorations, and balloons transformed the city auditorium into a magical wonderland. Carly felt like a princess. She and Leif danced and joked throughout the evening.

Afterwards, they rode in the limousine to The Sterling. Nervous, Carly could barely keep her hands still. As they made their way to the room, Carly's legs felt heavy, like she was fighting a current that threatened to drag her out to sea.

In the room, Leif turned on the radio to a local jazz station that played romantic songs all night. Then, turning to her, Leif leaned down to give her a gentle kiss. As he touched her skin, Carly jumped as though she'd been burned. "You all right?" Leif asked in confusion.

"Yeah. Sure. I . . . um . . . think I need to use the restroom," Carly responded. Then she backed away and walked into the bathroom, closing the door behind her. Staring at her reflection, the feelings that she had kept at bay for the past few weeks rushed to the surface, leaving her overwhelmed. *What am I doing here? I'm not ready for this. I don't believe in this.* Tears sprang to her eyes. *I want to wait for my honeymoon. I want to wait for my husband, even if it takes years and years. I don't want this—a couple of hours in a hotel after my senior prom. What was I thinking?*

After drying her eyes and splashing water on her face, she mustered her courage and walked out of the bathroom. "I can't do this," she whispered to Leif from the edge of the room.

Leif turned to look at her with a stunned expression. "What do you mean you can't do this? Do you know how much I paid for this room? I saved up for it for weeks."

"I know, Leif. I'm sorry. I thought I was ready, but I'm not. I don't want to have sex until I'm married," she said sadly.

"Well, what if we fool around doing other things and not have regular sex?" Leif said, as if trying to find a compromise.

Carly shook her head. "If you're talking about oral sex or anything like that, I still don't want to. It's still a type of sex and I'm just not ready."

Rolling his eyes, Leif responded angrily, "You should have figured that out before now." When Carly didn't respond, he grabbed his jacket and the picnic basket and stormed out of the room, banging the door on the wall as he went.

Numb, Carly slowly gathered up her purse and walked out the door. Tears began to fill her eyes. She willed herself to swallow the lump in her throat. *I'll cry when I get home. I don't know what I was thinking, God, but I'm glad You wouldn't let me go through with it.*

Remembering all the warnings that she'd faced in the last few weeks, she knew that God had protected her from making a huge mistake. *Thank You, God. Thank You so much.*

TRUTH LINK:

Dear Lord, please help me to be strong when it comes to sexual temptation. You know what it's like nowadays. I want to abstain from all kinds of sex, but I need Your help. Please show me who I should be around and who I should date. Amen.

POWER UP:

Everywhere we look, we're surrounded by sex. People on TV shows joke about it. Movies show it. Advertising sells things with it. It's portrayed as casual, something to be expected in any dating relationship. But the truth is, sex is special and spiritual. God wants you to enjoy it within the boundaries of marriage. He isn't punishing you by dictating that sex should be saved for marriage. Instead, He's protecting you from a lot of hurt. By saving sex, you won't be at high risk for unwanted pregnancies, HIV, venereal diseases, and endless broken hearts. You won't be filled with regrets about relationships that went too far too quickly. Instead, you'll know the spiritual and physical fulfillment that comes from experiencing sex with your spouse. Regardless of whether you're a virgin or not, make the decision today to save sex—all kinds of sexual activity—for marriage.

TURN ON THE LIGHT

Encouragement

DOWNLOAD:

God . . . has given me a well-taught tongue, so I know how to encourage tired people. He wakes me up in the morning, wakes me up, opens my ears to listen as one ready to take orders.

Isaiah 50:4 THE MESSAGE

Lena took her seat next to the window in the coach portion of the airplane. She stuffed her backpack under the seat in front of her and excitedly watched the airline workers load the suitcases and direct the other planes. She was on her way to visit her grandparents at their ranch, and she couldn't wait to get there. Each summer her dad sent her to visit them so she could ride horses and "stay in touch with her roots," as he put it. As an architect, he had to live in the city, but Lena knew he missed the country. She knew it was important to him that she love it too, and she did. She dreamed of being a veterinarian with a farm and animals someday.

Next to her, a woman sat down. She moved quickly and decisively. Everything about her—her tailored suit, coiffed hair, pearl jewelry, and Louis Vitton handbag—screamed Serious Business Woman. *She's probably a corporate lawyer,* Lena thought as she looked down at her own jeans and sweatshirt, suddenly feeling like an unpolished little kid. The woman adjusted her seat, pulled a large file folder out of her briefcase, and shoved her things under the seat in front of her. Then she began to read her documents, oblivious to everyone around her.

Definitely a lawyer, Lena thought as she glanced at the formal looking documents the woman read.

Turning her attention back to the workers outside the plane, she felt the excitement she always experienced when she flew. She loved it. She knew that many people hated to fly, but she loved the thought of soaring through the air, crossing the country in a matter of hours and seeing people from all over the world. Glancing around at the other passengers—all different ages and races—she wondered, *Where are they going? Where are they from? Why are they traveling? Are they, like me, going to visit family or are they on business?* Lena loved to imagine their stories. Looking over at the grandmotherly type sitting in the seat across the aisle, she imagined she was on her way to visit her new grandbaby. And the techie-looking guy next to her was probably on his way to a Star Trek convention. *Oh yeah,* she thought, smiling to herself, *definitely a Trekkie.*

After takeoff, Lena retrieved her CD player from her backpack and settled back for a quiet ride. A while later, the flight attendants came around with drinks and lunch. Lena removed her earphones and unwrapped her turkey sandwich. Then the woman next to her introduced herself as Maggie.

"What music are you listening to?" Maggie asked.

Swallowing a bite of her sandwich, she choked out, "*Beveled.*"

"I'm not familiar with them," she responded as she opened her chips.

"They're a new Christian band."

Maggie slid a surprised glance toward Lena. "You're a Christian then, huh?" When Lena said yes, the woman made a quick face. "I'm not religious myself. I can't convince myself that there's a god up there who knows my name. It all seems like fantasy."

Lena smiled but didn't respond immediately. She thought back to a time when she'd have agreed. She'd gone to church on Christmas and Easter, but it was all repetition and fables. Then she'd seen the truth. "Once I would have agreed with you," she said simply, "but then I realized there is a God who cares. It changed my life."

Maggie gave her an appeasing smile. "And what changed your mind?" she asked, as though waiting for Lena to reveal some trivial approach to life.

"My mom died," Lena said quietly. "No one could comfort me—not my family, not counselors, not friends. No one. Then one day I prayed and it felt like a blanket of love fell over me. And I couldn't get something I had heard at church one Easter out of my mind, so I went back. It was like Someone turned the light on inside me."

Maggie stopped eating while Lena spoke. Then she continued eating her lunch in silence, as if she were considering what Lena had said.

Lena didn't see herself as an evangelist, and she didn't share her faith with every stranger she met. But if prompted, she would talk about it. Jesus had changed her life. She was convinced of it. She hadn't grown up in Sunday school, knowing all the ins and outs of Christianity. Instead, she'd come to her faith with nothing. Other than the Easter and Christmas sermons, she didn't know anything. So when her life changed, when she finally felt alive again after her mother's death, she knew it was real. There was no other explanation.

"Do you think God hears your prayers?" Maggie asked quietly.

Lena noticed that Maggie no longer looked like the no-nonsense businesswoman she had earlier. Instead, she looked uncertain and even fearful. "Yes, I do. He doesn't always answer them the way I want, but I believe He hears and answers them."

Maggie sat quietly, as if she were considering Lena's answer. "You know where I'm going? To my father's funeral."

"I'm so sorry," Lena said gently.

"It's okay, really. We didn't get along. He wasn't around much when I was growing up, but I guess . . . I guess I hoped we still had time to work things out."

Lena didn't know what to say. She knew this woman was hurting. "Maybe you should try praying about it."

TRUTH UNPLUGGED:

Your words can bring healing in difficult situations.

The woman turned to her and then, with a shake of her head, dismissed it. "He wouldn't hear me anyway."

"You might be surprised. Like I told you, it changed my life. If you want, I'll pray with you," Lena offered. Lena watched as tears came to the woman's eyes, and she said that would be okay.

Lena gently grasped the woman's hand and closed her eyes. She prayed that the woman would have peace and comfort through her difficult time. She prayed that God would help her have closure with her father in her heart, and then she prayed that she would realize that Jesus loved her.

When they finished praying, Maggie wiped the tears from her eyes. For the rest of their flight, they talked about their lives. Lena told her about her summer vacation and her grandparents' ranch. Maggie told her about her high-rise apartment and career. After the flight, Lena and Maggie said good-bye. Lena promised to continue to pray for Maggie. As she joined her grandparents, she felt that she'd just made a friend. Although they probably wouldn't see each other again, Lena knew they'd both shared an important moment. Lena had been there in Maggie's time of need. Realizing that God had put them next to each other on that flight was just one more reason Lena believed.

TRUTH LINK:

Dear Lord, help me to see places where I can encourage others. I want to be sensitive to others when they need to hear that You love them. Amen.

POWER UP:

Have you ever found yourself in a situation where you wanted to encourage or help someone through a difficult time, but you weren't sure what to say? It happens to everyone. Sometimes the person in trouble needs you to listen, offer support, or do something for them. In those moments, don't underestimate prayer. Sometimes your sympathy and advice aren't the best remedy. Even if you don't pray out loud, you can still pray silently that God will give you the words to say. As you ask God for the words to speak, you will be a tool He can use to help a person in trouble.

THE GRACE TO LIVE AT HOME

Difficult Parents

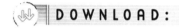

DOWNLOAD:

You have turned for me my mourning into dancing; You have put off my sackcloth and clothed me with gladness.

Psalm 30:11 NKJV

"Molly, where are you?" her father bellowed as he walked through the door. "Why isn't dinner ready? You're worthless. I work all day and all I ask is that you keep the house from looking like a pigsty and get a decent meal on the table. Worthless." He threw his jacket across the dining room table, covering the dishes that were set for dinner.

Hearing him, Molly stopped doing her homework and returned to the kitchen to finish dinner. "All I have to do is make the gravy. I was waiting for you," she countered. She knew it didn't do any good, but sometimes she couldn't help fighting back just a little.

"You gettin' smart with me? I put a roof over your head and make sure you have food to eat, and you want to smart off to me?" He eyed her, ready for a fight.

Molly could tell he was in one of his moods and it probably wouldn't improve. The best she could do was stay out of his way. Without saying a word, she finished the gravy and fixed their plates. Then, sitting down at the table, they began to eat. After a few bites, her father shoved the plate away. "Can't you make a simple meal without it tasting like garbage?" Taking the plate to the sink, he threw the dinner down the disposal and tossed the plate on the counter with a clatter. "I'm going out. Have this place cleaned up by the time I get back."

Numbly, Molly finished her meal and cleaned the kitchen. She knew the signs. By the time her father returned, she needed to be out of sight. Two years ago, her mother had left them. Molly still didn't know why her mother hadn't taken her too. That fact still stung. Her father had always been difficult. He was angry most of the time, yelling at, or even hitting, whoever was closest. That's what tonight was—a get-drunk-and-hit-something night. Molly actually preferred that he leave, although he would probably end up at the corner bar. Maybe he'd take his anger out on someone down there or be so tired when he came home that he'd go straight to bed. Most of the time, she could handle him. And when things got too bad, she either slept at a friend's or outside— anywhere he couldn't find her. Usually, by the morning, he'd either forgotten or dismissed anything he'd done the night before.

As the evening passed, she finished her homework and prepared for the next day, laying out her clothes and picking out what she'd make for tomorrow night's dinner. She worked after school, so she had to prepare everything beforehand so she could quickly move from one thing to the next the following day. She also took time to clean the bathroom and vacuum. Looking around the living room, she decided to dust and clean the windows later. All in all, the house looked pretty good. At least her father wouldn't explode over it.

The next morning before school, her friend Anna met her at her locker, "Hey, a few of us are going to a concert next weekend.

There'll be a few bands there—Charged and Effervescence. You've heard me play their CDs. Do you want to go?"

Molly considered it. "How much does it cost?" she asked. She had to be tight with her money. Though she made money at her after-school job, most of it went into savings for college. She had about $40 in spending money. Though she'd planned to go shopping for a new shirt this weekend, maybe the shirt could wait.

"Only $25." Anna answered. "Come on; it'll be fun."

Anna constantly invited Molly to Christian events with her other Christian friends, and Molly always had fun when she joined them. Most everyone was really nice and always made her feel welcome. "I'll think about it," she said.

After school Molly went to work waiting tables at a downtown diner. She worked there from 3:00 PM to 6:00 PM each weekday and also every other Saturday.

TRUTH UNPLUGGED:

If you have difficult parents, God can change their hearts and give you the grace to live with them. However, if you find you can no longer live there, ask God to guide you to someone who can help you make another choice.

Although the pay wasn't great, she made a good amount in tips from the professional types.

Later at home, she set the table for dinner and emptied the chicken and rice from the slow-cooker. Her father arrived home around 7:00 PM. each night. They sat together at the dinner table, although Molly didn't know why, since they rarely spoke. She just knew if she didn't have the table set and dinner ready, her father exploded. He constantly reminded her that "it was the least she could do."

"Dad, my friend Anna asked me to go to a concert this Saturday." she began carefully. It's a Christian concert so it won't be wild or anything. I wouldn't be here for dinner, but I'd make sure yours was ready."

He didn't respond for a few seconds. His head bowed toward his plate, he continued eating. "Waste of money" he grunted. "I ain't payin' for it."

"I have money. It's really not that much." When he didn't respond after a few minutes, she asked, "So can I go?"

"I don't care what you do," he responded as he rose to leave the table. "Just don't come home drunk, stoned, or knocked up. And if you get thrown into jail, don't call me." Then he left the kitchen.

On Saturday, Molly enjoyed the concert. Though she didn't know the songs, she still enjoyed screaming, clapping, and dancing with the rest of the crowd. At the end of the last band's set, the lead singer invited anyone who hadn't made Jesus their personal Lord and Savior to go to the front to pray with someone. He said that Jesus loved each person just the way they were, and because of that love, Jesus had died for their sins. All anyone had to do was accept His love, renounce their old ways, and live their life for Him.

Molly didn't understand everything the singer said, but she knew she wanted to know the kind of love he spoke about. Suddenly, before she could think, she moved into the aisle and walked toward the front. A college girl named Sarah met her, hugged her, and prayed with her. Unable to believe the peace and love that swept over her, Molly began to cry. All the pain that she'd buried deep inside came to the surface. She felt the pain of when her mother left her. She felt the sting of her father's harsh words. She felt the hurt of feeling so alone—unloved and unwanted. She felt the wound of so much responsibility all the time. As all the pain came to the surface, she felt some force sweep it all away. The longer she stayed, the lighter she felt.

Afterwards, Anna hugged her. "I'm so glad you went down there and prayed. I've been praying for you for a long time."

"You have?" Molly asked in amazement.

Anna nodded. "I know things aren't easy for you, Molly. You never say anything, but I can tell. It's good that you don't have to handle it all on your own anymore."

Molly smiled and nodded. "That's really nice to know."

The rest of the evening passed uneventfully, but Molly couldn't remember when she had been so happy. She chatted with the others on her way home. When she walked into her house, she heard her father's slow, steady breathing coming from his recliner. He'd fallen asleep in front of the TV. Watching him sleep, Molly knew he hadn't changed, but the dull numbness she'd felt was gone. Now, she just felt peaceful, and that was a very good thing.

TRUTH LINK:

Dear Lord, You know what my home is like. You know when it isn't loving or peaceful. I pray that You will continue to work in my parents so that one day they will come to know You. Until then, I pray that You will give me the grace to live with them. Amen.

POWER UP:

Wouldn't it be nice if everyone had a loving family who listens, loves, and wants the best for each other? Instead, you may live in a difficult situation. Your parents may be drug addicts or alcoholics. Someone in your home may be physically or verbally abusive. First, you need to decide whether you can continue to live there. If it's so bad that you need to leave, get help from a school counselor, pastor, or other adult. Or, you may need God's grace to help you live there. Remember, only God can change your parents' hearts, and even then, they must make the decision to allow God to change them. Until then, continue to pray for them. Ask God to help you live with them and find supportive Christian friends you can turn to. Don't believe that your parents' actions are your fault. Don't be ashamed or feel that there must be something wrong with you. There isn't. God is working on your behalf. He created you. He loves you, and He wants to help you.

SHATTERED INTO A MILLION PIECES

Heartbreak

DOWNLOAD:

If your heart is broken, you'll find God right there; if you're kicked in the gut, he'll help you catch your breath.

Psalm 34:18 THE MESSAGE

Kathryn felt the hot tears well up in her eyes as she closed her front door.

How could he do this? she thought as the tears began to stream down her face. *What went wrong?*

She and Daryl had dated for six months. Everything had been wonderful. They had met at school in the same world history class. She hadn't thought much of him at first, but then they'd worked on a class project together. She'd discovered that he was kind of outdoorsy, really nice, and funny. He'd asked her to go fishing and they'd had a blast. Kathryn found that she really liked his friends too. They were a lot like him. They weren't jocks, or brains—just regular guys who liked to hunt and fish. Kathryn liked that.

He was the first guy she'd ever fallen for—totally head over heels. At first, things had been exciting and new, but over time, they'd fallen into a really nice pattern in their relationship. They both loved God. They like canoeing, hiking, and watching adventure movies together. Daryl was even teaching her to rock climb. And since Kathryn saw herself as a bit of a tomboy, they were the perfect match. Everyone said so.

That's why the breakup was such a shock. Kathryn thought they were happy together and hadn't seen it coming at all. This was just their usual Friday night date. Then over a pizza Daryl had said the unthinkable.

"Kathryn, we need to talk," he'd said uncomfortably. "Um, I think we should break up."

"What?" She shook her head. Surely she hadn't heard him right.

"I just think we should see other people," he said.

Stunned, she'd stammered and tried to get him to give her a reason. Was he seeing someone else? Was he mad at her? What?

He'd danced around her questions, which made her mad. "Who is she?" she'd demanded. Then, she'd accused, "You've been cheating on me!" After several minutes of back-and-forth arguing, she'd stormed out of the restaurant. They'd driven home in silence.

She replayed the whole night over and over in her mind, unable to think of any reason for the breakup. She just knew she felt as if her heart had shattered into a million pieces.

"Katie, are you okay?" her mother asked with concern when Kathryn had come through the door.

"Fine!" she spit out and then ran to her room.

After slamming her bedroom door and crawling up in her bed, Kathryn buried her head in her pillow and cried. Oh, how she hated to cry, but she couldn't stop herself.

After a while, she heard a tap at her door. "Katie, can I come in?" her mother called gently.

Normally, Kathryn wouldn't have opened her door, but she found that she didn't have the strength to refuse. "Come in," she said weakly.

Over the next several minutes, she recounted the evening's events. In the end, her mother hugged her and said, "I'm so sorry. But trust me; he won't be the last guy you'll ever love."

Kathryn knew her mother was trying to encourage her, but she didn't want to hear that right now. She and Daryl were perfect for each other. She couldn't imagine not dating him.

The following Monday, Kathryn slipped into world history and took her seat behind Daryl. She couldn't even look at him. On one hand she hated him for breaking her heart, and on the other, she had to admit that he still looked good. In the past, he would have turned around and joked with her before class, but today he slouched down in his seat with his nose in his books, refusing to make eye contact with her.

With hope that they would chalk the whole thing up to a simple misunderstanding, Kathryn felt crushed all over again when at the end of class Daryl bolted out the door without giving her a glance.

As she dragged herself to her next class, Christina Myers stopped her. "Hey, did I hear right—you and Daryl broke up?"

Realizing the grapevine was already at work, she stood a little taller. "Yeah, we decided to see other people," she said flatly, refusing to give anyone the benefit of seeing how hurt she was.

Christina smiled, "Wow, I didn't think you guys would ever break up. Well, see ya."

As she walked away, Kathryn had the distinct feeling Christina was happy she and Daryl had broken up. She and Christina weren't close friends, but they knew each other. Now, Kathryn wondered how many other girls would be happy Daryl was "back on the market." Ugh! The thought made her sick to her stomach.

A few weeks passed, and with each day Kathryn felt a little less hurt and not quite so angry. She still missed Daryl, and she hated the fact that she no longer had a set date every Friday. But she was surviving. She started to hang out with some of her girl-friends again, realizing that she hadn't been as attentive to her friends when she and Daryl were an item. She had been too wrapped up in him to spend time with other people.

Then, she heard that Daryl and Christina Myers were dating. It didn't matter that she and Daryl weren't dating anymore; but Kathryn couldn't stand the thought of him dating someone else. Though they still sat next to each other, they hadn't spoken since the breakup.

TRUTH UNPLUGGED:

Trust God to heal your broken heart. Remember, He's interested in everything that concerns you— even your relationships.

Kathryn fought the fear that she'd never date again. What if no one ever asked her out again? What if Daryl was the only guy she was ever going to date and now he didn't want her?

Unable to get her head clear, Kathryn prayed, "Lord, please help me get over this. I don't know what happened with Daryl. Maybe it was timing, or maybe he just didn't love me like I loved him. I don't know. Right now, I just need to know I'm not alone or a loser and that Daryl won't be the only guy I will ever date."

As the weeks rolled by, Kathryn found the sting of Daryl dating again not quite so painful. Before when she'd seen him and Christina in the halls together, she'd gone the other direction. Now, she passed them without feeling sick.

"Hey, Kathryn, how are you doing?" Jeffrey Sherwood asked one day as Kathryn waited outside the school for her mom to pick her up.

"Hi, Jeffrey," she responded. Daryl had introduced her to Jeffrey when they were still dating. He and Daryl were friends—

not super-close, but they sometimes hung out in the same group. Jeffrey always made a point to talk to her whenever she'd been around. He was really nice.

"Listen, some of us are going waterskiing this weekend out at Poplar Lake. Do you want to go?" he asked.

Kathryn hesitated and then smiled. "That sounds like fun," she said.

"Cool. I'll pick you up at ten on Saturday. Maybe afterwards we can get some pizza at Lorenzo's." He smiled when she said she'd see him then.

Just then, her mother pulled up. Kathryn said good-bye and got into the car.

"Who was that?" Her mother asked. "He's a cutie."

"Jeffrey," Kathryn said, watching through the car window as he walked away. "He just asked me to go waterskiing this weekend and then out for pizza."

"That sounds like a fun date," her mother said.

Surprised to realize that she had a date, and even more surprised to realize she was looking forward to it, she turned to her mom. "Yeah, it does sound like fun." Turning back to the window, she smiled. So Daryl wasn't the last guy to ask her out. And better yet, God had answered her prayer. She was no longer hung up on Daryl. God really had helped her get over it.

TRUTH LINK:

Dear Lord, I really hurt right now. My heart is broken. Please help me to get past the hurt and show me that I'll have a successful relationship in the future. I know You want only what's best for me, and I trust You with my life—especially who I love. Amen.

POWER UP:

Have you had your heart broken? Have you been disappointed by love? Maybe you've dated someone who broke up with you. Or maybe you care about someone who doesn't share your feelings. Regardless, God wants to heal your heart. Sometimes we think that God is interested only in "spiritual" things, but in reality, God is interested in anything that concerns you. He wants you to trust Him with your whole life—even your broken heart. If you're in a place where you don't know how to get past the hurt, ask God to give you perspective and remind you that you will love again. Then look for Christian friends who can help you have fun and get your mind off your pain. In time, and with God's help, you will recover.

MAKING THE TIME COUNT

Attitude

DOWNLOAD:

A cheerful disposition is good for your health; gloom and doom leave you bone-tired. Proverbs 17:22 THE MESSAGE

"Hi, welcome to The Sub Shack. What can I get you tonight?" Ashley asked through the microphone.

"I'll have a large roast beef sub with everything on it, a bag of chips, and a medium Coke," the faceless customer ordered.

Ashley gave the customer the total and then made her way to the preparation bar to make the sub sandwich. Oh, how she hated this job. She needed to work and The Sub Shack was one of the only fast-food joints that closed on Sundays so she could still go to church with her family. At first, she thought it would be cool since she liked the sandwiches, but now, just the sight of a huge slab of processed lunch meat made her sick, not to mention the smells—onions, pickles, jalapeño peppers. And then there was the sticky film from the soda fountain that covered the floors and counters. She hated that too.

She had decided to get a job because she needed gas money for her car, to buy clothes, and to go out with her friends. Now, most of her nights were either spent working or catching up on homework from the nights when she had to work. It was a vicious circle.

Why couldn't I have just been born wealthy? she wondered constantly.

"Ashley, do you have that roast beef sub ready yet?" her manager Chuck asked.

Ashley slopped the makings on the sandwich and started to wrap it up. "Yeah, I got it," she said halfheartedly.

Chuck walked over. "Hey, how about making that a little neater?" he said in exasperation.

"What does it matter? They'll never know."

"Trust me; it matters," Chuck said shortly. "Now straighten it up or make a new one."

Ashley gaped at him and rolled her eyes as she unwrapped the sub. The contents tumbled out every which way. Ashley shook her head and mumbled under her breath, "It's just a stupid sandwich. Like anyone cares what it looks like."

At the end of the night, Chuck approached Ashley and announced, "Hey, Ashley, I need you to come in at two on Saturday. Melanie can't work on Saturday and Dwayne can't get here until six. Can I count on you?"

Ashley looked at him. "But I'm not supposed to come in until four."

"I know," Chuck said as he made notes to the schedule, "but I'm shorthanded and I need you to come in earlier."

"Why can't Melanie work?" Ashley asked in frustration.

Chuck stopped writing on the clipboard and turned to Ashley, "She had a family function to go to. She asked for that time off."

"Fine," she said flatly and walked away. She could feel Chuck watching her but she didn't care. It's not that she had plans on

Saturday afternoon, but she didn't want to have to come in early either. *This is ridiculous,* she thought.

The next week, when Ashley arrived at work, she noticed a new face. "Ashley, this is Trey. He's new." Ashley smiled and said her hellos. The guy looked nice enough.

As his shift wore on, Ashley noticed Trey working really hard. He swept and mopped the floors, straightened the vegetable bins, scrubbed the soda dispenser, and unpacked new supplies. "You can slow down, ya know?" Ashley said. "This isn't a marathon."

"I just don't like standing around. I like to keep moving," Trey said as he went to wipe down the dining area tables.

After working a couple of shifts together, Ashley noticed that Trey's zeal hadn't let up. Trey still outworked everyone else. *Knock yourself out,* Ashley laughed inwardly.

The following week, when Ashley reviewed the upcoming schedule, she noticed that she'd been scheduled for only three nights instead of her standard five. *Finally,* she thought, *I can get out of this place.*

Though she enjoyed her downtime, she felt frustrated when her paycheck came. It was almost half of what it had been. *Oh no!* she complained inwardly. *How am I going to have enough money for gas and going out?*

Over the next few weeks, her scheduled hours decreased even more. One week, she was down to two nights and only a couple of hours on Saturday. What was going on? Frustrated, she approached Chuck about it. "Hey, Chuck, what's up with my hours lately? I need to work."

Chuck gave her a small smile. "I thought you'd be happy to be working less. It doesn't seem you want to be here anyway."

"What do you mean?" Ashley challenged. "I'm here when I'm supposed to be."

"Yeah, you're here," Chuck said flatly, "but you're either complaining or doing just enough to get by. You don't take pride in your work; you throw the sandwiches together. You're short with the customers, and I have to *ask* you to do anything extra."

Ashley looked away as her face started to turn red. As much as she hated to admit it, everything Chuck had said was true. She never put herself into her work.

"Look, Ashley, I know this is just a job to you, but I need people who want to be here. I need people who want to work and have good attitudes while they're doing it."

"Are you firing me?" Ashley asked in amazement as the thought of getting fired gripped her heart.

"Not yet, but if you don't want to be here, then you need to go somewhere else. To be honest, I need people who are more like Trey. He comes in on time, he's pleasant, and he works hard. And he doesn't give me an attitude if I ask him to do something extra—like come in early. Right now, it's your choice. You can stay and work yourself up from the bottom of the list, or you can go."

TRUTH UNPLUGGED:

Don't let a bad attitude ruin your relationships with your family, co-workers, or friends. Trust God to help you gain a more positive outlook on life.

Ashley hung her head and quietly answered, "I'd like to stay." After Chuck walked away, Ashley felt sick. How embarrassing would it have been to be fired for a bad attitude? Her parents would have flipped at that. And how would she have responded at a future interview when they asked her why she'd left The Sub Shack? That would have been awful.

Thankfully, she still had a job, but she wasn't going to make much money now since she'd get only the leftover hours. She had to start fresh and get busy. Turning to the preparation station, she noticed the tomato bin was low. Heading back to the large refrigerator, she decided, *I better make my time count.*

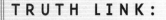

TRUTH LINK:

Dear Lord, I have really been frustrated lately about things in my life. Help me to deal with the situations with a good attitude. Sometimes I just can't help letting my irritation show. Help me to control my attitude and have the wisdom to do what I need to do. Amen.

POWER UP:

Have you ever been accused of having a bad attitude? Do you sometimes think people just don't understand? It's true. People may not always understand what's troubling you, but be careful about allowing your concerns or irritations to continually flow onto others. Put yourself in their place; would you want to be around someone who is constantly in a bad mood? What would you eventually think about that person? Even if the person doesn't say anything, you can tell when someone doesn't want you around. Of course, everyone needs space at one time or another—yes, even your parents and other family members—but when you need time to yourself, be respectful about taking it. If you're struggling to have a positive attitude, ask God to help you and begin to read your Bible. Not only will it give you great perspective on your life, but it'll also remind you of all the things you have to be thankful for.

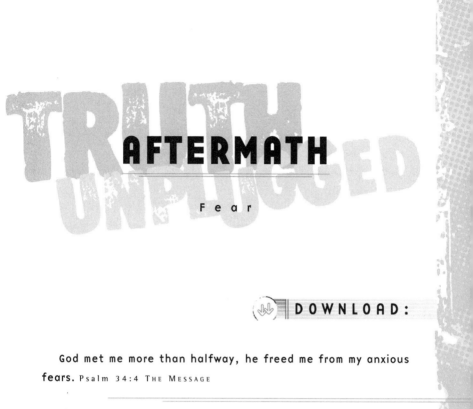

AFTERMATH

Fear

DOWNLOAD:

God met me more than halfway, he freed me from my anxious fears. Psalm 34:4 THE MESSAGE

"Hey, John, can I have a small popcorn and a medium diet soda? And can I have a box of Hot Tamales?" Shae asked. Boy, working at a cinema really had its perks. She had started working there a few months before, and now she was able to see movies for free and get a discount on her snacks. It was so cool!

Since her late afternoon shift had just finished, she ran to the bathroom to change out of her uniform and then rushed to the concession stand to buy her snacks before the new horror film started.

"Come on, Shae. You're gonna miss the beginning," Lance urged.

Grabbing her snacks, Shae raced to the screen. There on the fourth row was her group of friends who worked at the theater. They'd all just finished their shifts and decided to see *Revenge II* together.

Shae was so excited. She'd never seen a horror film in the theater. Her parents really didn't like her watching them. They said horror movies played tricks on your mind, causing fear. Shae's sentiments were: "It's just a movie."

Why do they still treat me like a little kid? she wondered in disgust. She was sixteen now. She had a job and her own car. So what if they helped her buy her car; she still made the payments on it and took care of it. She was an adult now. They didn't need to shelter her anymore.

"Augh!" Shae screamed as the faceless killer jumped from behind the barn door, grabbing the unsuspecting teenage girl by the throat. Hearing her cry, Shae's friends laughed.

Then in the final scene, as the hero finally defeated the killer, Shae watched in horror as blood squirted everywhere. Unable to watch anymore, she closed her eyes. It was too disgusting.

After it was over, her friends jumped up, "Man, that was cool! Didn't you love how the blood dripped down the wall at the end?"

"And didn't you love how the killer dragged that one victim into the marsh, leaving a trail of blood and body parts?"

"That was so cool!"

Shae felt numb. She'd never seen anything like it before. Trying to act like it wasn't so bad, she joined in the banter.

As they walked out of the theater into the darkness, Shae's friends turned to the right and headed to their cars. Shae's car was at the far left end of the lot. After saying her goodbyes, she tried to walk to her car without freaking out. She couldn't help it; after what she'd just seen, she was nervous. In fact, she ran the last twenty paces to her car, threw open her door, jumped inside, and hit the automatic locks. She looked around trying to shake the feeling that someone could be following her. Thankful that she didn't see anyone, she pulled out and drove home.

Later that night, Shae sat straight up in bed out of a dead sleep. Turning to the clock, she saw that it was only 3 o'clock in the morning. Sweat trickled down her back and she gasped, desperately trying to catch her breath. She'd had a bad dream and she could still see it in her mind. She'd been running, trying to get away from the Revenge killer. She'd tried to escape through the swamp, but her feet were stuck in the mud. She could see him coming closer and closer, but the harder she struggled, the more stuck she became. That's when she woke up.

After catching her breath and splashing water on her face, Shae tried to fall back asleep. In the pitch dark, she couldn't relax. She continued to imagine that something else was in her room. The reflection of the moonlight on the tree branches outside her window danced across her blinds, giving the effect of fingers. She pulled her sheets a little closer and finally had to plug in her nightlight so she could fall asleep.

TRUTH UNPLUGGED:

Refuse to dwell on fearful images
that steal your peace of mind.

In the morning, she woke from a fitful sleep. Making her way to the kitchen, her mother saw her tired expression. "Shae, are you okay? You look really pale." She moved over to place the back of her hand on Shae's forehead. "You're not running a temperature, but you sure don't look like you feel well." Shae mumbled that she hadn't slept well and moved to the kitchen to get a cup of hot tea.

After school, Shae clocked in at work and took her place at the concession stand, still exhausted from her bad night's sleep. She dragged herself through her shift.

"Hey, Shae, do you want to stay late for another movie tonight?" Lance asked at one point. "We're going for a repeat performance for *Revenge II*. It was so cool; I can't stop thinking about it. I just have to see it again."

"Yeah, I keep thinking of it too," she responded with a nervous laugh. "Thanks, but I think I'll pass." There was no way she was going to sit through another performance of *that* freak show.

Later that night as she turned to switch off her bedroom light, she hesitated. She really wasn't looking forward to another sleepless night. She'd already run to her car again on the way home and jumped whenever someone called her name.

Desperate for some peace of mind, she prayed, "Lord, I get it. I understand what my parents meant about not watching horror movies. Please, please, please erase that movie from my mind."

It took a few weeks, but eventually, Shae began to forget the movie. Whenever a scene came to her mind, she prayed for God to erase it. And whenever she felt like someone was stalking her, she prayed for peace. When Lance asked her to join the group at the next horror movie, Shae kindly declined. She knew what it would do to her peace of mind and it wasn't worth it.

TRUTH LINK:

Dear Lord, I have images in my mind from horror shows or books that stay with me. Please help me to not only remove the images from my head, but also the fear in my heart. In the future, I'll stay away from those images and forms of entertainment. Amen.

POWER UP:

Have you ever thought it was cool to be scared—either by a movie, book, or TV show? Afterwards, have you found it difficult to get the images or impressions out of your mind? Come on; be honest. You can probably still remember the first horror show you ever saw. Maybe at the time, you found the fear thrilling, but the truth is, it steals your peace of mind. After reading or watching those images, do you find yourself afraid of things? Do you find yourself looking over your shoulder when you're alone at night? By dwelling on images that make you afraid, you train yourself to be afraid. If you're afraid because of things you've watched or read, make the decision to stay away from that form of entertainment. Then, ask God to help get the images from your mind and get rid of the fear. Remember, as thrilling as you may think horror or fear is, nothing is worth surrendering your peace of mind.

IT'S NOT A DATE!

Manipulation

(🔽) **DOWNLOAD:**

"Just say 'yes' and 'no.' When you manipulate words to get
your own way, you go wrong." Matthew 5:37 THE MESSAGE

"Billy, you're so funny," Haley said pushing his arm. "You
always make me laugh." Haley loved joking with him. They were
biology lab partners. Since Haley hated dissecting worms and
frogs, it was nice to have Billy there to do the disgusting parts.
Haley jokingly referred to herself at Billy's lab assistant.

"Hey, Hale," Billy said, using the nickname that only he called
her, "are you going to the baseball game this weekend?"

"Maybe. Are you asking me to go?" she cooed.

"Maybe. I'll pick you up at 5:30."

After class Haley made her way to her next class. She sat
down next to her friend Christy and began unpacking her notebook and papers.

"Do you need a ride to the game this weekend?" Christy
offered. She was dating Jimmy Knowles, the pitcher. She never
missed a game.

"No, thanks. Billy's gonna take me," she answered.

"Billy? You're going out with Billy?" Christy asked in amazement. Haley knew Christy liked Billy. He wasn't the best-looking or most popular guy in school, but he was the class clown and smart.

"Date?" Haley cried. "No, it's not a date. We're just friends. He's my lab partner in biology. That's all."

"Are you sure he knows that? Cause I've heard that you guys are pretty cozy in class together," Christy asked skeptically.

"Of course he knows that. We just joke around."

The next day in the hallway, another of Haley's friends stopped her. "Hey, Haley, I heard you're going out with Billy this weekend. Is it true?"

"We're *just* friends," she responded in frustration. Why were people talking about her and Billy as if they were a couple? Sure, he was nice, but she would never consider dating him. He just wasn't her type. She was much more interested in tall, athletic types. Of course, she was going to the Friday night name with him because she needed a ride, and he was funny and harmless. In fact, she hoped that she could talk to Steven Foster, the shortstop, at the game. Now, he was an interesting prospect.

On Friday night, Haley took special care getting ready. She wore her new capri pants with a short top that showed a hint of skin. As she walked out of her bedroom, her mother looked at her and asked, "Do you think that outfit is really appropriate?"

"Mom!" Haley wailed, "all the girls are wearing clothes like this. It's no big deal."

Her mother shook her head, "But don't you have a date?"

"It's not a date. We're just friends. He's giving me a ride; that's all." Her mother continued to look uncertain as Haley left with Billy.

At the game, Haley and Billy took their seats in the stands. "Do you want anything to eat or drink?" Billy asked shyly.

"No, thanks," Haley said as she scanned the field looking for Steven.

"I'm really glad you said yes," Billy said. "I really didn't think you would."

"Oh, it's fun hanging out with you," she said, nudging him with her shoulder.

After their team had won the game, Haley excused herself to go talk to Steven. She had such a good time talking to him that she completely forgot about Billy. Finally, Billy walked up beside her. "Haley, are you ready to go?" he asked gruffly.

Surprised at this tone, Haley responded, "Sure, Billy. I'll be right there." Then she excused herself from Steven and followed Billy back to the car.

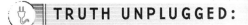

TRUTH UNPLUGGED:

Treat people with respect and honesty instead of allowing yourself to try to manipulate and control them.

Once inside, Haley turned angrily to Billy. "What's your problem? You had no right to talk to me like that in front of Steven."

"No right?" Billy said tensely. "You're on a date with me and you're flirting with him?"

"What are you *talking* about? This is not a date. We're friends; that's all," she spit out.

Billy looked at her like he'd been slapped. "What are *you* talking about? I asked you out and you accepted. You've flirted with me all year. I just finally got the nerve to ask you."

"I accepted going to a school baseball game with a friend. And I do not flirt!" Her voice rose to a scream.

Matching her tone, Billy yelled, "You've flirted with me all year. If you were any more obvious, you could charge admission. Ask anyone."

Haley was so angry, tears filled her eyes. "Take me home," she demanded.

Replaying the awful scene in her mind all weekend, she felt sick. Deciding she needed to talk to someone, she called Christy and recounted everything. To her surprise, Christy was less than sympathetic. "What did you expect, Haley? He asked you to the game. He picked you up. And I'm sorry, but you *have* flirted with him all year. I've seen it and I've heard other people talk about it."

It was Haley's turn to feel like she'd been slapped. "I didn't mean to lead him on," she said plaintively.

"Come on, Haley. You can't tell me you didn't like the attention, and the fact that he did all the work for you in biology," Christy reasoned.

Haley listened in silence. She was glad Christy couldn't see how red her face was. It was true; she couldn't deny it. She did flirt with Billy to get him to do her work, and she did like the attention he gave her. "People really talk about me like that?" Haley asked quietly.

"Yeah, they really do," Christy responded softly. "I'm sorry Haley, but everybody knew you were just playing him."

After Haley hung up the phone, she cried. She cried because she had lost Billy as a friend. She cried because she had stupidly used him, and she cried because she saw herself for what she was—a user. She'd embarrassed Billy and herself. She knew that she would have to apologize to him; they still had biology together. But she also knew she'd have to start paying attention to her actions. They obviously affected more people than just herself.

TRUTH LINK:

Dear Lord, please forgive me for manipulating people. I realize that I need to treat them with respect and be honest with them. Thank You for showing me when I begin to manipulate them, and please show me how to act responsibly at all times. Amen.

POWER UP:

Have you ever tried to get someone to do something or act a certain way, but instead of saying exactly what you want, you schmooze and flirt to control them? Maybe you let them think you'll be great friends. Or you let them believe you have romantic feelings for them. Inside you know you're being dishonest because you only want to get them to do what you want—you use them. Although you may get them to do what you want in the short run, people will eventually think of you as a Master of Manipulation, and that's a dangerous title to have.

ANYTHING I WANT

Lying

Truth lasts; lies are here today, gone tomorrow.
Proverbs 12:19 THE MESSAGE

Valerie called the yearbook meeting to order. "We have a lot to discuss this week. So let's get started," she began. "First, we have to come up with a theme for the yearbook, and then we need to decide how to handle senior pictures. So does anyone have any ideas for the theme?"

It was Valerie's first year as yearbook editor. After working on it for the past two years, she finally had the chance to make it her own. She was so excited to meet with the rest of the yearbook team and hash out the details. Bantering ideas back and forth, the team grew passionate. Several wanted to base the theme on a popular song. Others wanted to base it on current events, and one or two threw out ideas that were completely off-the-wall.

Valerie loved the creative process, but the meeting also helped her get an idea of her team's strengths. Kathy, another yearbook veteran, was very creative. Then Sam and Mike were great photographers—very visual. Debra loved to write, so her ideas were geared towards puns and play on words. Then there was the newbie—a freshman named Jeri. Jeri had worked on her junior high yearbook so she had some experience, but Valerie thought she was still new to the whole process. She had a lot to learn.

After the meeting, Jeri approached her. "Valerie, I wanted to run an idea past you. My uncle is a photographer in town, and he's willing to do some really different shots for the seniors this year. He lives on a farm with a lake and he can do some great outdoor shots." Then handing Valerie a stack of photos, she added, "He took these of me last year. He's really good."

Valerie flipped through the photos. They were good—really different than the typical senior photos. They looked more like photos out of a fashion magazine. He'd incorporated the lake as a background and had taken beautiful shots of Jeri among wildflowers. "These *are* good," she admitted. "But we already use Bryson Photography. We have for years."

"Yeah, I know, but maybe we could give the students a choice. My uncle did say he'd give the students a great deal."

"Okay, let me talk to Mrs. Glenn, our sponsor, about it," Valerie said, handing the photos back to her.

Within a few weeks, the yearbook was in full swing. The staff began to lay out several ideas for spreads. They would come up with the theme, start getting the clubs involved in planning their pages, and receive orders for advertisements. Valerie had started to feel the pressure of bringing everything together on time and under budget.

One day, Jeri went up to her and said, "Hey, Valerie, have you talked to Mrs. Glenn yet about using my uncle?"

Valerie stopped. It had completely slipped her mind. "No, I haven't talked to her about it yet. I'll talk to her this week. Sorry, I gotta go." She turned and rushed down the hall. Valerie didn't mean to blow Jeri off, but she was way too busy to think about Jeri's photographer uncle.

Over the next few weeks Jeri asked Valerie several times about using her uncle. Each time, Valerie dodged the question. It wasn't that she had anything against Jeri or her uncle, but Jeri's pushiness was wearing a little thin. This was her first year working on the yearbook. Why couldn't she just let it go? They already had a photographer. Sticking with the regular photographer would simplify things. And right now Valerie needed things simple.

At one of their weekly meetings, Jeri asked again if Valerie had discussed the matter with Mrs. Glenn. Exasperated, Valerie responded, "Yes, we're sticking with Bryson Photography. Let's move on." Jeri looked at her with a stunned expression, her mouth slowly forming in an angry, straight line.

A couple days later, Valerie was working late in the yearbook room when Jeri entered. "I need to talk to you," Jeri said flatly.

Valerie looked up. "Okay. What's up?" She could tell Jeri was angry.

"Why'd you lie to me?" Jeri asked hotly with her hands on her hips. "You said you'd talked to Mrs. Glenn about using my uncle as a photographer and you never did. I know because I talked to her about it today and she thinks it's a great idea."

"You went behind my back?" Valerie asked in surprise.

"Well, I didn't like your answer. There was no reason for it. Bryson Photography is lame. The students complain about them every year, so why not give them a choice?"

"How do you know the students complain every year? You're a *freshman*," Valerie shot back.

"Oh, I get it. I can't have an opinion because I'm just a lowly freshman. Well, that's stupid, Miss Yearbook Editor. I'm on this team too," Jeri said angrily. "And just for the record, it doesn't take a brain surgeon to know Bryson Photography is lame. I have two older brothers. They went to Bryson Photography for their yearbook photos and then to my uncle for the ones they gave away. Everyone loved the ones my uncle did."

"I really don't care if your uncle is the best photographer in the world. It's easier to use one photographer. We're using Bryson," Valerie said with finality.

"Really? Well, Mrs. Glenn will be calling you about that and about the fact that you lied about talking it over with her," Jeri said crossing her arms. "And you can bet that I'll be showing my uncle's photos to the rest of the yearbook team."

"I'm the editor. I can do anything I want."

"Anyone who'd rather lie than think about what's best for the students isn't fit to be editor," Jeri said, storming out of the room.

Valerie was shaking. Though she'd stood strong in front of Jeri, she crumbled

TRUTH UNPLUGGED:

Lying destroys relationships. It drives a wedge between the person who lies and those who hear and believe the lie.

afterwards. She hadn't *meant* to lie about meeting with Mrs. Glenn, she'd just gotten tired of Jeri asking her about it. The truth was, though, Jeri was right. Valerie hadn't given her credit for coming up with a good idea simply because she was a freshman. And instead of following through on what she said she'd do, she'd allowed herself to take the easy way out—she'd lied. Now she was going to have to face Mrs. Glenn.

The following day, Mrs. Glenn confronted her about lying to Jeri and not taking Jeri's idea seriously. She talked to her about good leadership and telling the truth—even in difficult situations. Mrs. Glenn told her that it was up to her to work this mess out since she'd caused it. Mrs. Glenn also warned that if she wasn't up for the challenge of being yearbook editor, maybe she should resign.

Valerie promised that wasn't the case.

Walking into the yearbook meeting the following week, Valerie stood at the front. She could feel the tension around the table. Jeri had already told people about her fight with Valerie and Valerie's lie. She had also shown her uncle's pictures to them. The senior class buzzed with excitement at the chance to have their pictures taken by him.

Nervous, Valerie began to speak, "I'm sure everyone has already heard about the addition of the new senior photographer. The senior class will have the choice to use Jeri's uncle for their senior pictures." Then, stopping to take a breath, she continued, "I also need to apologize to Jeri for not being honest with her last week. I said that I'd talked to Mrs. Glenn about using her uncle when, in fact, I hadn't. I just got busy with everything and it slipped my mind. Then when she put me on the spot, I said I had. I'm really sorry."

As the meeting continued, the tension eased. Valerie made a point of listening to the ideas of everyone around the table. She was surprised to realize that Jeri had several good ones. Afterwards, Valerie pulled Jeri aside to apologize again. Jeri accepted her apology, though Valerie knew it would be awhile before Jeri forgot the incident. *So much for being yearbook editor,* she thought as she watched Jeri leave. *I guess I can't do anything I want after all.*

TRUTH LINK:

Dear Lord, please forgive me for saying anything less than the absolute truth. Even when it seems easier to lie, help me to be honest. Amen.

POWER UP:

Have you ever been in a situation where it seemed easier to lie, or fib, than to tell the absolute, 100 percent truth? Everyone has. Though lying may seem like the easiest answer at the time, it can come back to haunt you. As someone lies, it becomes easier the next time and the time after that. Then one day the truth comes out and the lie is exposed. After that, it takes more time and energy to build trust in those to whom you lied. When it comes down to it—it's not worth it. Though the truth may be difficult in the short run, it will save your relationships and self-respect in the long run.

BIG BIRD, CHUBBY, AND OTHER FRIZZ

Image

DOWNLOAD:

God created man in his own image. Genesis 1:27 NIV

"Hey, Sarah, you goin' tubing down the river with us on Saturday?" Pastor David asked as soon as she walked into youth group.

"No, I don't think so," she said offhandedly, trying to look unconcerned.

"Why not?" he cried in amazement. "We're gonna have a blast."

"Um . . . well, I have some homework that's due next week and . . . well, I really need to stay home to get it done," she lied, while inwardly praying *God, forgive me.*

Hesitating a second, as if reading her mind, he said, "Well, I hope you'll change your mind. It won't be the same without you." Then he turned to talk to a couple of other kids who had just arrived.

The truth was, there was no way Sarah was getting into a bathing suit in front of her youth group. She pretty much avoided any situation that required her to bare any more leg than a skirt or at the very least really long walking shorts. It's not that she was fat—exactly—but as her dad always said, "You have your grandmother's big bones."

Usually she was okay with her size, but she wasn't a glutton for punishment. Sarah could still remember being called Chubby in elementary school and Big Bird in junior high. And she wasn't looking for a repeat of those days.

I can just imagine, she thought, *one tubing trip would surely give me yet another name to live with throughout high school. With my luck, it'd end up listed under my senior yearbook picture with the rest of my accomplishments and goals, and I'd be forever thought of as the big girl who went tubing and floated down the river without needing an inner tube.*

True or not, the mental picture alone was enough to keep her on dry land.

As youth group started, Sarah took her seat next to her friend Amanda. Amanda was petite with china doll skin and beautiful curly auburn hair that hung halfway down her back. As the music started thumping, everyone got to their feet and began singing.

"Are you going on Saturday?" Amanda asked between verses.

"Yeah, right. Not a chance I'm getting into a bathing suit in front of this group" Sarah shot back.

"Yeah, I'm not sure about going either," she said looking back toward the stage.

"Why not?"

"My hair. It kinda looks like I stuck my finger in a light socket when it gets wet and dries without smoothing lotion in it."

"You're kidding, right? Your hair is beautiful," Sarah said, straining to be heard over the music as the beat picked up.

"Thanks, but it takes a lot of work to keep it tame."

They went back to singing and focusing on the band, but Sarah couldn't quite concentrate on the song. She couldn't get over the fact that Amanda didn't want to go because of how she might look.

Wow, what a shock! She's gorgeous and still self-conscious, Sarah thought. She would have never guessed it by looking at Amanda.

As the songs came to an end and everyone took their seats, Pastor David took the stage with his Bible in hand. "Okay, everybody, listen up. I was gonna continue our study of Moses, but as I was praying about the service today, the Lord took me in another direction. Everybody open up to Genesis 1:27. Now, I wanna ask you something." He waited while everyone turned in their Bibles, and then he continued. "We all know that we're not supposed to say rude things to other people, right?"

We all nodded in unison and a few yeah's were thrown out as Pastor David paused for a response.

"So why do we think it's okay to talk down to ourselves?" he asked.

Everyone sat there wondering what he meant.

"How many of you—and don't raise your hands because we've all done this at one time or another—look in the mirror and think that you're not good-looking enough or not cool enough or smart enough or athletic enough? Or how many of you have actually thought, 'I'm such a loser'?"

He waited for his words to soak in and then continued, "If we said those things about someone else, we'd all agree that we'd be outta line. But you know what? Thinking or saying that about yourself, about someone God created, is outta line too. You are His creation, and just like the old saying goes, 'He don't make junk.'"

Pastor David kept talking, but Sarah didn't hear him. She thought about all the times she had looked at herself in the mirror and thought, *Chubby* or *Big Bird*. How many times had she called herself those names? Some kid years ago had called her that once or twice, but she'd called herself that almost every day since.

All of a sudden Amanda nudged her. "I guess I'm going tubing," she whispered.

"You are?"

"Well, yeah. Like this message wasn't just for me. Here I am not going on the tubing trip because of what I think people will say. I'll take my chances with someone else calling me Frizz Top. I just need to quit calling myself that."

"I know what you mean," Sarah said lowering her gaze to her hands.

"So are you goin?"

Weakly, Sarah looked up at Amanda and gave her a small smile. "Sure, why not? If I lose my nerve, I'll wear a T-shirt over my bathing suit, right? But at least it's a start."

TRUTH UNPLUGGED:

Out of everyone who has ever lived or who ever will live, God's purposely made you just the way you are—with a unique combination of His attributes.

TRUTH LINK:

Dear Lord, please forgive me for having cruel thoughts about myself. I realize that You created me and You didn't create me lower than anyone else. You love me just the way I am. Help me to see myself the way You see me. And help me to forget all the harsh things that people have said about me in the past. I realize that what they said isn't the truth. You created me in Your image and Your image is perfect.

POWER UP:

Do you say or think cruel things about yourself that you couldn't imagine saying to someone else? Then why would you say them about yourself? You can change that. Dismiss any negative talk and begin to think good things about yourself: what you like, what you're good at. You are God's creation. He hasn't made you ugly or stupid or clumsy; He's made you in His image. He's given you special talents and abilities that are unique to you—that's how much He loves you. Instead of looking at yourself and wishing you were different, look at yourself and thank Him for all that He's given you. Then every day, remind yourself that you are His creation and He loves you just the way you are.

GET OUTTA MY LIFE!

Sibling Rivalry

DOWNLOAD:

Love is patient, love is kind. It does not envy, it does not boast, it is not proud. It is not rude, it is not self-seeking, it is not easily angered, it keeps no record of wrongs. Love does not delight in evil but rejoices with the truth. It always protects, always trusts, always hopes, always perseveres. Love never fails.

1 Corinthians 13:4-8 NIV

"Where's my white sweater?" Elena demanded as she stormed into the kitchen, glaring at her sister who sat at the breakfast table enjoying a bowl of Cheerios.

"I don't know," Eva responded.

"I know you have it. It was in my closet last week and now it's gone. I haven't worn it and you're the only other person who would wear it. Hand it over," Elena barked at her.

"I don't have your stupid sweater!"

"Mom, Eva stole my sweater," Elena called to her mother who stood in the nearby utility room emptying clothes from the washing machine into the dryer.

"I did not!" Eva yelled back.

"Girls, stop yelling," their mother said. "Elena, your sister said she doesn't have it. Eva, finish your breakfast. You're both going to be late for school if you don't hurry."

"You always take her side," Elena wailed, storming out of the kitchen.

For as long as she could remember, Elena had dealt with her sister's irritations. They were only eighteen months apart in age and she couldn't remember a time when Eva wasn't there. And since Eva was the baby, their mother always took her side. Eva could do no wrong, whereas Elena was older and had to be more responsible. That was what her mother often said, and Elena was sick of it.

School was the only place Elena got relief from her sister. There, they were in different grades—two years apart—and had different friends. Elena hung out with her friends on the girls' basketball and volleyball teams, while Eva was on the drill team. Their paths didn't cross very often.

"Hey, Elena, can I get a ride home from school with you and Sybil?" Eva asked in the hallway between classes. "Mom can't pick me up and she told me to get a ride home with you."

"No, I have basketball practice until 4 o'clock. Find another ride," Elena said.

Eva looked frustrated. "Please, Elena, I need a ride. I'll wait."

"I said no."

"Why do you always have to be so mean? Like I ever did anything to you," Eva responded.

"Give me a break. You're always in my way. I swear, I wish you would just get outta my life," Elena shot back and stormed away.

After school Elena attended basketball practice and then rode home with her friend Sybil. When she walked through the doorway, the house was quiet. Elena got a drink from the kitchen before sitting down to do her homework at the kitchen table. At 6:00 P.M., her mother walked in with her arms full of bags.

"Will you and your sister help me unload the groceries?" her mother asked as she set the first load on the counter.

"Sure, I will. I don't know where Eva is," Elena said, closing her trigonometry book and rising to go out the garage door.

"What do you mean you don't know where she is? Didn't she come home with you?" her mother asked, turning to face her.

"No, she got another ride." Elena shrugged.

"I told her to get a ride with you. What happened?"

Elena huffed. "I told her I had practice and she needed to get another ride."

Her mother stared at her with wide eyes. "You refused to give her a ride? It's 6 o'clock, she's still not home, and you stand there with an attitude? Get on the phone right now and find your sister." Her mother sounded tense. Elena could tell she was on the verge of losing her temper.

TRUTH UNPLUGGED:

Your brothers and sisters need to see as much, or more, kindness, love, mercy and patience, from you as anyone else you meet.

Elena huffed again and stalked to the phone, dialing Eva's best friend. After five phone calls, she still didn't know where Eva was. After ten phone calls, she started to run out of ideas and began to worry. Where was Eva? Why hadn't she found a ride and come straight home?

"Any news?" her mother asked glancing at the clock; it was 6:30 P.M.

"No, several people say they saw her after school, but no one could give her a ride home. They haven't seen her since," Elena answered.

"I'm going to look for her," her mother said, grabbing her keys and heading out the door. "Oh, and call your father and let him know."

Elena continued to call anyone she could think of. Her sister was missing and she was responsible. If she hadn't been so mean, Eva would have been home with her hours ago. Now, her mother was out frantically looking for her. "God, please bring my sister home safely. I'm sorry I was mean to her. I'll do better. Just please bring her home," she prayed.

At 7:00 P.M. her mother walked in with Eva. Elena ran to her and threw her arms around her sister's neck. "Thank God. Where have you been?"

"I was at the school helping Ms. Watson with the signs for the game this weekend. She said she'd bring me home after we finished since I didn't have a ride. Time just got away from me. I'm sorry I didn't call, Mom," Eva said, turning to her mother.

"We'll talk about it later. Right now I want you to go unload your stuff and clean up for dinner. I want to talk to your sister," their mother said. After Eva left the kitchen, she sat down at the table and motioned for Elena to join her. "I called your dad and let him know she is okay. Elena, it has to stop, now!"

"What?" Elena said, though she had a good idea of where this was going.

"You are so angry at your sister all the time. You don't even see her as a person. And today your actions could have had serious consequences. Now, Eva is responsible for not calling, but she wouldn't have had to look for another ride if you hadn't been so mean to her when she asked you for a ride. You are not the only one in this family."

Elena looked down at the table. "I know, Mom, but she's always in my way. And you always take her side on things. School is the only place I don't have to share with her."

Her mother nodded, "That's true. But it's also the only place she doesn't have to share with you either. And I don't always take her side on things, but honestly, you blow up so fast whenever it comes to your sister that I try to smooth things over rather than let her catch it from both of us. You have zero patience when it comes to her. She's not perfect, but neither are you. You just need to ease up with her."

Elena nodded reluctantly.

"And by the way, I found the white sweater that you were so sure your sister had stolen. It was at the bottom of your closet. It had fallen off its hanger." After watching her a few seconds, her mother rose to begin dinner.

Elena continued to stare at the table. She felt so ashamed. She'd really been cruel to her sister. Sure, Eva could be irritating, but maybe she had been just as irritating at her sister's age. *Thanks for bringing her home safely, God,* she prayed silently as she rose to set the table. *Just like I promised, I'll make more of an effort to be nice to her.*

TRUTH LINK:

Dear Lord, please help me to show Your love—Your grace, Your mercy, Your kindness—to my brothers and sisters. Help me to be the best sister I can be. Amen.

POWER UP:

Have you ever noticed how difficult it is to show the love of God to your brothers and sisters? It's true. They can get into your stuff and razz you over the littlest things. They know just which buttons to push to make you angry—and they push them better than anyone. Showing them patience and kindness can be hard, but well worth it. As irritable as they may be, remember that no one can ever take their place. You understand each other better than most because you've grown up in the same family, regardless of whether you're full, half, or stepsiblings. In time, hopefully, you'll be able to celebrate each other's gifts and talents instead of focusing on each other's failures and weaknesses.

WE'RE IN THIS TOGETHER

Illness

Young women will dance and be happy, young men and old men will join in. I'll convert their weeping into laughter, lavishing comfort, invading their grief with joy. Jeremiah 31:13 THE MESSAGE

"Melanie, are you going to the hospital to visit your mother today?" her father asked. Melanie noticed how tired he looked. Dark circles shadowed his eyes, and his shoulders slumped in a way they never had before.

"I don't know. I'll have to see," Melanie said before heading out the door to school.

Her mother recently had had surgery and treatment for cancer. Since then, Melanie's dad had practically lived at the hospital. Every day, he asked if Melanie would go to the hospital too, and every day Melanie said she'd have to wait and see. Melanie knew she should visit more often, but she just couldn't. She couldn't stand to see her mother so sick and weak. She'd lost her hair and quite a bit of weight. She had a pale, ghostly look about her. Melanie almost didn't recognize her.

She remembered vividly how her parents had sat her down to tell her that her mother was sick. "Melanie, the doctors found a lump in my breast. They've done a biopsy and it's malignant. I have to go into the hospital for a mastectomy and chemotherapy treatment. Now, I don't want you to worry. We'll get through this," she'd said it so calmly, but Melanie knew the truth. She was staying strong for her and her dad.

As she spoke, Melanie noticed her father staring off with a blank look on his face. He'd always been a sturdy, you-can-count-on-me sort of guy, but Melanie sensed that he was struggling. Melanie knew this wasn't as simple as her mother had made it sound. The only thing she knew about cancer is that her grandmother had died of it years ago, but Melanie had been so young that all she could remember was her mother crying when her grandmother had died. Her mother looked so healthy, so strong, and fit. Melanie couldn't fathom how she could be sick.

The day of her surgery, she and her dad had sat with her mother until they wheeled her into the operating room. She'd made jokes trying to ease the tension, but Melanie couldn't be soothed. She watched as a processional of people from their church visited. Several tried to console her with words such as: "God knows best." Or "Your mom is in God's hands now." She didn't want to hear what they had to say. In fact, the more they spoke, the angrier she became. They didn't understand what she was going through. Her mother was about to go into surgery for *cancer,* such an ugly word. She was Melanie's mother. She didn't belong to them. They didn't know her mother like Melanie did. They didn't love her like she did. They couldn't possibly know what was going through her mind.

Since the surgery would take quite awhile, she'd decided to take a walk. She couldn't just sit in the waiting room as the walls closed in around her. Walking up and down the halls didn't help.

She saw all kinds of sick people and smelled all sorts of strange, strong, clinical smells. All of it made her skin crawl. Inwardly, she screamed, *God, why did this happen? Why is my mother going through this?* And then she begged, *Please help her. Please don't let her die.*

After the surgery, she and her dad had sat in the hospital room. She'd watched her dad watching her mother and stroking her mother's hand. She'd always known her parents loved each other. They were affectionate around the house and, much to Melanie's embarrassment, still went on dates. But as she watched her dad, she saw how difficult this was for him. Seeing her father in such pain only intensified her own.

They'd found another tumor under her arm, causing her to have a second surgery. After that, Melanie had only visited the hospital once. She had been shocked by her mother's sickly appearance. Since then, she hadn't been back. She just couldn't take it.

Driving to school, she began to pray again for her mother, "Lord, please heal my mother. Please let the surgery and treatment work so she can come home and be healthy again." As she prayed the same words that she'd prayed a hundred times every day since she'd been told the news, she felt strange. She pulled her car into a parking lot. Then, as if a dam had broken, she wept for the first time. She let it all go—all the pain and all the fear. She wasn't sure how long she sat there, but finally her tears began to dry up and she knew what she had to do.

Turning her car around, she headed to the hospital. Like a robot, she walked through the lobby, entered the elevator, and pushed the button to her mother's floor. She smelled the same smells, but she didn't stop. For the first time, she wasn't afraid. Entering her mother's room, she stopped. Her mother was still so small, but she didn't let the sight scare her. *She's my mom,* she repeated over and over again in her head.

Walking to the side of her bed, she took a seat and gently took her mother's hand. She opened her eyes, focused on Melanie, and smiled, "Hey there."

"Hey, Mom," she said with tears in her eyes. "How are you feeling today?"

"I'm actually feeling better today," she responded slowly, closing her eyes.

"It's okay, Mom," she said. "You sleep. I'm here and Dad's coming. It's going to be okay. We're going to get through this. We're all in this together."

She watched as her mother gently nodded her head and drifted off to sleep.

Still holding her hand, she bowed her head again and began to pray, "Okay, Lord, I'm here and I'm not leaving. I need her to be healed and home with me and Dad. And just like I know You haven't given up on her, I'm not going to either."

TRUTH UNPLUGGED:

When an illness strikes your family, God can give you courage and strength to face the situation. Ask Him.

For the first time, she felt the courage and determination to make good on her prayer. She realized what she'd said to her mother was true. This was a family thing—the hardest they'd ever faced—and they were all in it together.

TRUTH LINK:

Dear Lord, I have a loved one who is ill and I need You to help us through this. I rely on You as their Healer—because I know You can and will heal. And as you work on their behalf, will You also show me how to deal with this? Give me the wisdom, courage, and peace to handle this situation. Amen.

POWER UP:

When illness strikes your family, it affects everyone. If you've faced this, you know how true that is. Everyone does their best to handle the situation, but it's still difficult to know what to say or how to act. You may get angry or pull away, trying to deny that anything's wrong. Or you may feel depressed. You may turn into Superwoman, trying to handle everything that needs to be done. Whatever the situation, take time to pray. Lean on Jesus, and ask Him to show you what to do and how to handle things. Ask Him for healing, strength, and courage. You're not alone; He's there with you.

GETTING THE WHOLE STORY

Criticism

DOWNLOAD:

Those people are on a dark spiral downward. But if you think that leaves you on the high ground where you can point your finger at others, think again. Every time you criticize someone, you condemn yourself. Romans 2:1 THE MESSAGE

"Hey, Janna, where's the popcorn? We're ready to start the movie," Logan called from the living room where Janna's closest friends had gathered for their Friday night movie-fest.

"It's coming. I'm getting drinks. Who wants regular and who wants diet?" she called back. "And who wants to help me get them?"

Marcy jumped up and ran to the kitchen. "I'll help. By the way, is John coming?"

"You know him, he's always late," Janna said.

Janna and Marcy carried trays of sodas, popcorn, and chips into the living room where everyone grabbed their favorite spots. Janna sat on the floor hugging a big pillow. Logan stretched out in the recliner. Marcy and David took the couch. That only left a spot for John, who usually sprawled out on the floor. They were all set for their *Indiana Jones* marathon.

"Should we wait for John?" Logan asked.

"Yeah, let's give him a few minutes. He should be here anytime," David piped up.

"You guys, he's always late. We shouldn't wait on him," Janna reasoned, grabbing a handful of popcorn. "Now that he's got that new pizza delivery job, you just can't count on him. He should have gotten off 30 minutes ago, but with him, you just can't tell."

"I don't think he's *always* late," Marcy said, eyeing Janna. "He just needs a little more time to get here since he started working. We have time; let's wait.

Janna shrugged. She didn't necessarily mind waiting for John, but it irked her that he wasn't there when he knew they started the movie at 9:00 P.M. They had been meeting for Friday night movies for the last year. Each week, they voted on the movie for the following Friday, and if they couldn't decide, they drew titles out of a hat. It had been running smoothly until John got a job. His new schedule really threw a monkey wrench into their schedule.

After about five minutes, Janna grew impatient. She went to the phone and dialed his number. "Are you *ever* gonna get here?" she snapped into the receiver when he answered his cell phone.

"I'm on my way right now. I had a big delivery out on South Pine Street. I should be there in ten minutes," he explained.

"Fine. Just get here. We're waiting," she said into the phone before quickly hanging up.

Turning to the group, she found Marcy glaring at her. "Ease up, Janna. It's not like Indiana Jones is going anywhere."

Janna met Marcy's glare and took her seat on the floor again. "It just bugs me that he knows we start at nine and he's still not here. This has happened a lot lately." She didn't care what Marcy said; his lateness was getting out of hand. The other day, he was supposed to meet her at the music store at 6:00 P.M. and he didn't show up until 6:20 P.M. Then he was supposed to give her a ride to the hockey game last week and he was 30 minutes late. They'd missed the first goal. It was becoming a habit and she didn't feel she could count on him. He always apologized and even called to say he'd be late, but she didn't care. He was supposed to be there when he said he'd be there.

Ten minutes later, John walked in carrying a pizza. "Sorry, I'm late. I brought a pizza." He set it down on the kitchen table and collapsed onto the floor. "I'm so tired," he said. "We had a huge delivery out on South Pine Street. It took two cars to get it all there. I was supposed to get off an hour ago, but they needed me to help. I got a good tip though."

Janna went to the kitchen to grab paper plates and napkins for the pizza. Though she was always happy to have pizza, she was still irritated that John hadn't arrived on time. As she placed everything on the table and started dishing up the slices, the others talked about this and that: their days, John's job, the movie, the pizza, and other inconsequential things. She didn't join in their conversation; she was too irritated.

"Pizza's ready," she called with a slight edge in her voice.

They poured into the kitchen, grabbing paper plates and napkins. Janna stayed to the side, waiting for everyone to get theirs before getting her piece. Back in the living room, they

TRUTH UNPLUGGED:

Compassion from you may be the tool God needs to help someone in need.

all took their spots. Then Janna spoke up, "Do we still have time for the movie or do we need to choose something shorter?" she asked.

Everyone looked at one another and then at her. "I think we have plenty of time," Marcy piped up.

"Fine. Start it," Janna responded flatly.

Irritated, she drained her soft drink and rose to get a refill. In the kitchen, John joined her. "What's up, Janna? Why are you so angry?"

Slamming the freezer door, she turned on him. "I'm tired of always waiting. You know we start the movie at nine. Lately, you're never on time."

"I'm sorry. What else do you want me to say? I have a job now. I can't always control when I get off," he reasoned with tension in his voice.

"I don't *care* about your job," she said.

"Well, you may not, but I do. I'm not like you, Janna. My parents don't pay for everything. I have to work. If I don't keep this job, my parents will take my car away."

Janna stood there stunned. She didn't realize that's why he had to work so hard. She thought he just liked the extra money his job provided. Now, she felt like a jerk. She'd been so self-righteous about his being late because she thought he was dealing with the same things she was. Now, she realized there were special circumstances. "I'm sorry. I didn't know," she said quietly.

"Yeah, well, I don't advertise it. Most of what I make goes to pay for my car, so I sometimes try to pick up extra shifts to have spending money," he said. Janna nodded, finally understanding. John peeked around the corner at the television screen and then looked back at Janna, "Come on, let's go watch the movie. I promise I'll try to be on time from now on."

Janna smiled. "And I promise to be more understanding and not so critical."

John winked. "Great, come on. Let's go eat some pizza and watch Indie."

With the half-eaten pizza in hand, they returned to the living room, took their seats, and enjoyed the rest of the movie among their best friends.

TRUTH LINK:

Dear Lord, please forgive me for being critical of others. I know I need to be understanding and realize that I may not know everything about the situation or the person. Please help me to be compassionate and understanding. Amen.

POWER UP:

Have you ever found yourself critical of someone else—maybe a friend, a sibling, or even a complete stranger? Perhaps you think they should act a certain way or be something that they're not? When you criticize someone you become their judge, but you may not have all the facts. Maybe they're in a no-win situation that they're handling the best way they know how. Or maybe there's more to the story than they've told you. Or maybe they're responding to something based on what has happened to them in the past. Regardless of the reason, they need your under-standing. That's not to say that you should condone sin. You shouldn't. But instead of becoming critical, take your concerns to God in prayer. Then ask Him to help you be the best friend, witness, or family member you can be. Your understanding may be a tool that God uses to help a person in need.

GOT IT PRETTY GOOD

Thankfulness

DOWNLOAD:

Let the peace of Christ keep you in tune with each other, in
step with each other . . . And cultivate thankfulness.

Colossians 3:15 THE MESSAGE

"My parents are driving me crazy!" Heather said in frustration.
She'd just come from her house where she'd had another fight with
her parents. "They just won't get off my back about school. My mom
wants me to get a tutor for the SATs this summer. Isn't that crazy?"

"Why do they think you need a tutor?" Missy asked from the
flowerbed where she was pulling weeds. She continued working
as Heather ranted about her parents, something she often did.

"She's not sure I'll make high enough scores on my own to get
into Wellington. They require a 1200. Like I care about going to
Wellington," she said, pacing back and forth in front of the garage.
"They just hound me all the time. Why can't she just leave it alone?"

"Do you think you can get a high enough score on your own?"
Missy asked.

"I don't know. I just know I don't want to study this summer. I want a real summer. I want to go on the school trip to Europe. You know, the whirlwind trip, ten countries in 15 days. France, Germany, Italy. It'll be amazing! My parents say they'll pay for it only if I get a tutor for the rest of the time. Can you believe it?"

When Missy didn't respond, Heather looked down at what Missy was doing. Heather didn't know much about gardening, but Missy did. She was always weeding the flowerbeds or planting vegetables in their garden. Heather usually just stood around while she worked. Over the years, she'd come to recognize the difference between a tomato and a carrot plant, but that's about it. "So you want to go grab a pizza and go check out some new music at the mall?"

Missy peered up at her. "Sounds like fun, but I have some things to do around the house this afternoon."

Considering this for a minute, Heather offered, "What if I help you? We could get everything done fast and then go to the mall." Missy accepted Heather's plan, and they set out to finish Missy's list of chores as quickly as possible.

"Well, I need to mow and finish weeding the flower beds," Missy said.

Heather had mowed the yard at her house a few times and suggested that she start there. When Missy uncovered the push lawn mower, Heather scowled. "You mean you don't have a riding lawn mower?" Missy laughed in response and pushed it out to the driveway.

After checking the oil and the gas, she primed the motor, adjusted the carburetor and started the mower in one swift jerk. Heather stood back the entire time, realizing that she was on foreign turf. She'd never had to do any of that. Most of the time, her father mowed the lawn. Occasionally, they even had professionals come to help. Every once in a while Heather did it, but then all she had to do was sit on the back of a big riding lawn mower and turn a key. If it didn't start, she called her dad. No problem. This was different.

As she began pushing the mower around the yard, she noticed immediately that not only was the mower not a riding mower, but it didn't move easily. When they said push, they meant throw your weight against it, forcing it to move.

After mowing, she moved on to one of the flowerbeds that hadn't been touched yet. Looking around, she didn't see Missy anywhere. Imagining that Missy was off loafing while Heather did her work, she went looking for her. As she wandered through Missy's house, she heard a noise from the master bedroom. Peeking around the corner she saw Missy standing in the master bathroom tub with a plunger in her hands. "What're you doing?" she asked.

"My mom said her drain is clogged. I think I almost have it cleared," Missy said as she strained to plunge the drain.

"Why don't you just call a plumber?" Heather asked in confusion.

Missy laughed as she continued to strain. "Cause . . . this . . . doesn't . . . cost . . . anything."

Heather left to return to the yard where she crawled on her hands and knees pulling anything that didn't look like it belonged there. As she worked she thought about the differences between her life and Missy's. She'd never really considered it before. She knew that Missy's dad had left years before and that Missy didn't have anything to do with him. She knew that Missy's mom worked in an office downtown as a secretary. Although Missy never complained, Heather knew money wasn't as easy to come by for them. As far back as she could remember Missy had worked. She'd washed cars around the neighborhood when she wasn't old enough to get other work. Now, she waited tables after school and on weekends. Heather hadn't really thought about it before. She just figured Missy liked to work. Now, she wondered if Missy worked out of necessity instead of desire.

Piling her hair on top of her head and securing it with a clip, she walked back into the house. "What's next?" she asked, getting into the spirit.

"My mom wanted me to clean the outside of the windows and screens. Once we do that, we should be finished," Missy said looking around as if trying to remember if there was anything else.

Outside, they worked together. One removed the screens and washed them before returning them to their places. The other concentrated on cleaning the windows. As they worked, they talked about their upcoming senior year. "So where are you going to go to college?" Heather asked.

Missy was quiet for a while. "I'm not sure. If I go, it'll be to the community college."

"Community college?" Heather asked in surprise. "But you've got great grades. You can get into just about any school you want. Why stay at the community college?"

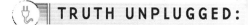

TRUTH UNPLUGGED:

Instead of looking at the things that aren't quite right in your life, focus on all the good things God has given you.

"I can get a scholarship and I can still live here with my mom. I've already got a job, and my boss said that he'd make me an assistant manager at the restaurant next year. I'll make more money, so I can help my mom out more. It just makes sense," she answered as she continued to work.

"But what about the whole college experience: living in the dorms, going to college games, dating college guys, all that?" Heather asked.

Missy shook his head. "That's not for me. I've got other things to think about: helping my mom, helping with my sisters, our house, making money. I don't have time for all that other stuff."

They continued working in silence. Heather couldn't believe how easy her life was by comparison. She and Missy had been friends for years, but she'd never acknowledged this side of Missy's life. She'd been too wrapped up in her own. She wouldn't even consider not going to college. It was just a matter of which one. Her parents wrote the checks. Even now, she thought of the argument she'd had with her parents earlier, which seemed to pale in comparison to Missy's life. Heather's parents offered to send her on a two-week trip to Europe that was surely going to cost a lot of money, but Heather had thrown a fit because her parents demanded that she study to get into a top-notch university first. All she had to do was make the grade; that's it. Other than that, her ticket was paid. *Wow,* she thought, *I really do have it pretty good.*

After they finished the windows, Heather was exhausted. She'd never worked so hard in her life. As they climbed into Missy's car, Heather turned to her friend, "You know, maybe we could just get the pizza and skip the mall. I don't think I could walk very far."

Missy laughed. "I think you're right. Thanks for helping me. You saved me a lot of time."

"No problem," she responded as they pulled out of the driveway, but she thought, *Thank you, you're the one who really helped me.*

TRUTH LINK:

Dear Lord, please forgive me for taking all the good things in my life for granted. Help me to see everything You've given me and keep an attitude of thankfulness. Amen.

POWER UP:

Do you ever catch yourself taking people or things for granted? Your family's love and advice? Opportunities? Choices you've been allowed to make? At one time or another, everyone forgets to look at the good things and instead focuses on the things that aren't so good. But God wants us to be grateful for all the good He's put in our lives. As we're thankful to Him and others around us, we'll be able to be better examples of His love to the world. And by focusing on all the good things in our lives, we'll be able to enjoy our lives even more.

WORTH MORE THAN THAT

Modesty

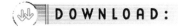

DOWNLOAD:

Don't drag your feet. Be like those who stay the course with committed faith and then get everything promised to them.

Hebrews 6:12 THE MESSAGE

Mia walked into the coffee shop after a long day of school and practice for High Steppers, a dance group at her school. At the end of a hard practice, she treated herself to a hot cup of non-fat cinnamon mocha cappuccino.

Being the captain of such a prestigious dance group was hard. She practiced long, but the reward was worth it. Her team had won the state competition for high school dance groups last year and was sure to retake the title this year. Of course, dance practice had its personal bonuses too. Because of it, Mia was in excellent shape. She worked out hard and held to a strict diet. Her body was toned, which was necessary for the High Steppers' spandex uniforms.

Not that she saved her figure just for the uniform. Mia loved to show extra skin whenever she could. Midriff shirts, ultra low-rise jeans, deep V-necked shirts, backless anything, short shorts, and mini-skirts were staples of her wardrobe. People complimented her physique, and she got lots of attention. She knew just how to play the game.

Standing in line ready to place her order, she spotted Riley Ferguson at a table, reading a book. Riley was the cutest guy in Fellowship of Christian Athletes. He was always leading some new crusade: fundraisers for group ski vacations, mission trips to Central America, outreaches to inner city kids, and more. Not to mention, he was a nice guy. Mia had tried to get to know him but she could never get past a casual acquaintance with him. As far as she could tell, he didn't seem interested. But maybe, she thought, she just needed to turn up the heat a little.

After placing her order, she went over to Riley's table, sat down and gently squeezed his shoulder. "Hey, Riley, I haven't seen you in a while," she said with just the right amount of honey in her voice.

"Oh, hi, Mia. How are you?" he said before returning to his book.

She noticed she'd lost his attention and decided on another approach. Pulling up a chair, she sat down and crossed her legs, putting them in the best light. "What are you working on?"

"History," he said, glancing her way before returning to his book.

Hearing her order called, Mia retrieved her drink and returned, determined to draw him into a conversation. "I just got out of practice. This is my reward."

He smiled and nodded.

"We're supposed to go to the state competition in two months, so we really have to push to get ready," she said, smiling her best smile.

Again, he nodded.

"So do you have a test coming up or something?" she asked.

"Yeah," he said. Then standing up, he added, "Well, I better get home. I'll see you later." Picking up his books, he left. Mia sat stunned. No guy had ever blown her off like that. She felt angry. Who did Riley think he was anyway? On her drive home, she determined she would have Riley eating out of her hand before it was all over.

At the next FCA meeting, Mia entered the group wearing one of her most flattering outfits: lace-up jeans with a tight, midriff T-shirt. Walking up to the group of guys Riley was with, she put on a dazzling smile, aimed right at Riley. The group of guys stopped talking and welcomed her. All eyes were on her. All eyes, that is, except Riley's. Once the attention turned to her and she started to work her flirtatious pats and toss her hair like a pro, Riley left. Mia felt the sting of his disinterestedness.

The next week she tried again, but this time she went for the romantic look, wearing a short, floral skirt with a peasant blouse that had a plunging neckline. Walking in, she joined his group, but instead of focusing on him, she focused on one of his friends. She wanted Riley to feel what he was missing, but within minutes, Riley abandoned the group–again.

What is his problem? she wondered. She was completely perplexed as to why he had no interest in her. It seemed that he couldn't seem to get away from her fast enough.

After the meeting, Mia went out to her car only to find it wouldn't start. Since almost everyone else had already left and she had forgotten her cell phone, she went back inside the building to call her parents. She reached the door as Riley was coming out. He glanced at her. "Did you need something?" he asked.

"Yeah, my car won't start," she said. "I think it's the battery. I was just going to call my parents."

"I have jumper cables in my car," he offered.

Mia agreed and they walked back to the parking lot. He hooked up the cables and started his car, and then Mia started hers. After a few minutes of letting her car charge, Riley detached the cables, closed both hoods, and got ready to drive away.

"Riley, can I ask you something?" she said before he got back into his car. She couldn't let him leave without knowing what it was about her that turned him off. "I was just wondering why you don't like me. You're nice and all, but I always get the feeling that you can't wait to get away from me."

Riley looked down first and then back up at her. "I'm embarrassed for you, Mia."

Mia scowled. "Embarrassed for me?" she repeated in amazement. "What are you talking about?"

Riley shrugged. "You dress like you just walked out of a Victoria's Secret commercial. You let people—especially guys—treat you like a toy. You play right into that image. It's sad," he said gently. "You deserve better than that."

Confused, she responded, "I dress this way because I think I look good and I can carry it off when other girls can't."

Riley nodded sadly. "I just think you sell yourself short. People would like you for yourself, not because you wear clothes that are too tight, short, low, or see-through." Then shrugging again, he added, "That's just what I think."

As Mia drove home she thought about what Riley had said. He was so off base it wasn't funny. She didn't sell herself short. She didn't let people treat her like a toy. Did she?

Over the next week, she watched how people, especially guys, treated her. She realized that most of the guys she thought of as friends looked at her as if she were a doll. They touched, squeezed, and patted her all the time. More often than not, they looked her up and down with looks that were overtly sexual. In the past, Mia would have been flattered, but after talking to Riley, she realized that she wasn't a person to them, but a piece of meat.

As the week wore on, Mia became increasingly uncomfortable in her clothes. She went shopping and found some really cute clothes that didn't show extra skin. In the past, Mia would have passed them by, but now she actually felt pretty in them.

The next week at school, Riley approached her. "Hey, Mia, how are you doing?" he asked carefully.

"Fine, thanks," she said as she started to leave, a little uncomfortable talking to him after their last conversation.

Instead of letting her make a quick exit, Riley fell into step beside her. "Are you okay after what I said last week? I really didn't mean to hurt your feelings, and I'm sorry if I did."

"It's okay. You were right," she said simply, still trying to get away. "I didn't realize it until you said what you did."

"Well, you look really nice tonight. In fact, I was wondering if you'd like to go get a cappuccino."

Mia stopped and turned to him in surprise and confusion. "Why?"

Riley shrugged. "I think we could be friends."

Mia cautiously agreed. Much to her surprise, they had a great conversation, and really talked—about God, school, dancing, missions, and more. It was probably the best conversation Mia had ever had with a guy. She didn't toss her hair, flirt, or flash any skin at all. And he didn't once look at her like a pin-up model. It was cool to know someone was seeing the real Mia—and seemed to enjoy her company. In fact, it was a whole new experience, one she hoped to enjoy again.

TRUTH UNPLUGGED:

God wants you to be treated with respect and kindness because of who you are, not because of what you look like.

TRUTH LINK:

Dear Lord, please help me to see myself the way You see me instead of following after the world's view of beauty. Help me to appreciate modesty even when those around me don't. Amen.

POWER UP:

In today's society, it's easy to think that wearing your clothes tighter, shorter, lower, and more invisible is beautiful. The image is all over magazines, television, and movies, but your beauty is not based on outward appearances. Of course it's nice to look attractive, but what's going on inside you is much more important. Don't try to fit into the world's mold of "beauty." You are more valuable to God than that.

UNLOVABLE

Suicide

 DOWNLOAD:

"This is how much God loved the world: He gave his Son, his one and only Son. And this is why: so that no one need be destroyed; by believing in him, anyone can have a whole and lasting life."
John 3:16 THE MESSAGE

Laura stood at the bathroom sink staring hopelessly down at the razor she held in her hand. Would she have the nerve to follow through with her plan? But then again, what was the alternative? Continue with life the way it had been? No, that wasn't an option.

She'd heard her parents argue about her. "Well, you're never around," her mother had thrown at her father. "You're supposed to take her every other weekend, but you cancel as often as you take her. I need time off too, you know."

"What? So you can be with the latest boyfriend you drag home? Give me a break," her father had shot back. "You're her mother, for God's sake. You can't expect me to make up for the mess you caused." Back and forth they went.

They'd been divorced for years. The only time they even spoke was when Laura had made a mistake or the child support check was late. Whenever it came to Laura and her problems, they reveled at pointing the finger at each other. Each thought the other was to blame.

Laura closed her eyes, thinking how nice it would be to not have to hear them argue anymore. She could be free. She wouldn't have to put up with anymore of her mother's latest flings hanging around the house and trying to buddy up to her. And she wouldn't be forced to sit through another drilling from her father about what she wanted to do with her life and how she needed to be decisive and work hard instead of wasting her time on frivolous, teenage things. Laura had always suspected that the pep talks had come from her dad counting the day until she turned 18—the day he could stop sending the monthly child support payment.

Not that she blamed them.

She looked at herself in the mirror. She admitted that she was unlovable. She tried to be the perfect daughter, but she couldn't help herself. She wasn't pretty. She wasn't smart. She wasn't witty. She didn't have many friends. "Who could love someone like me?" she said out loud to the reflection in the mirror.

Looking around the bathroom, she began to prepare. She didn't want there to be a lot for her mother to clean up, so she began filling the bathtub with water and gathering towels to catch any excess blood.

Will they miss me, she wondered, *even a little bit?*

Maybe her dad would miss a day of work for her funeral. Maybe he'd even turn off his cell phone, but at least he wouldn't have to send any more child support.

And what about her mother? Would she drag the latest loser she was dating to Laura's funeral? *I hope not,* Laura thought.

Then she stopped. What about Grandma Lil? She hadn't thought about her. Grandma Lil would miss her. Grandma Lil would miss her a lot. Sitting down on the edge of the tub she thought about the only person who made her feel loved—Grandma Lil.

She was everything a grandmother should be: warm, loving, strong, and smart. Laura loved visiting Grandma Lil on her farm. She was in her sixties, but she still kept a small farm out in the country with chickens, a garden, and even an old cow that she milked every day. When Laura was there, she always felt so safe. She helped her grandmother tend the garden and collect the eggs from the chickens and even milk the cow. And when they sat down to a garden-fresh, made-from-scratch meal, they always grasped hands and said grace.

Normally, Laura didn't go to church. It just wasn't something her parents had ever done. But when she was at Grandma Lil's, she couldn't imagine not going. Sitting in the small, old church, she felt just as warm and loved as she did when she was sitting in Grandma Lil's kitchen.

Laura loved those visits to the farm. They were few and far between, however. It wasn't that her grandmother lived that far away, but Laura's parents were usually too busy to take her, and Grandma Lil didn't like driving in the city. She said it made her too nervous.

TRUTH UNPLUGGED:

Suicide is never an answer to the hopelessness you feel; Jesus is.

Wondering what she should do, Laura decided that at least she should call Grandma Lil one more time, a last good-bye. Turning the tub water off, Laura went into her room and dialed the number.

"Laura," her grandmother cried into the phone after Laura identified herself. "How's my best granddaughter?"

"Fine, Grandma. I just wanted to call and say hi."

"You know, it's the strangest thing," her grandmother began, her voice taking on a serious note, "you've been on my mind all day. I've been praying. I asked God to take care of my grandbaby. Are you sure you're okay?"

Laura felt a lump rise in her throat. "Sure, Grandma, I'm okay," she choked out.

Her grandmother was quiet for a moment before answering, "Well, I've been thinking it's time for a visit. When can you come?"

"I don't know. I'll have to talk to Mom and see when she can bring me."

"Phooey. I'll come get you myself. When can you come?" her grandmother responded with determination.

"But, Grandma, you don't like driving in the city," Laura responded weakly.

"Don't you worry about that. I'll get one of my friends and we'll make a day of it." As Laura listened, the tears that she had held at bay began to trickle down her face, and try as she might, sobs caught in her throat. "Oh, Laura," her grandmother responded to her crying, "God sees you. He let me know that you needed your grandma. I love you so much. You don't even realize how special you are."

Laura could hear the emotion in her grandmother's voice and she felt her love coming right through the phone. "Now," her grandmother continued, "I want you to get that little Bible I sent to you last Christmas." Laura slowly rose to retrieve the little Bible from her bookshelf. "Open it up to the table of contents and find the book of John in the New Testament. Now, I want you to read the whole book of John. You'll see that Jesus loves you and He died for you. You are not alone. He's right there with you." Laura promised to read it. Then her grandmother added, "I'll call your mother right now and make arrangements to pick you up tomorrow, so you be ready."

After Laura hung up the phone, she felt more hopeful than she had in a long, long time. Pulling open the Bible, she began to read. As the story unfolded, Laura felt a peace come over her that she hadn't ever sensed before. After finishing one page, she went on to the next, eager to find out the rest of the story. Slowly, she realized she wasn't so unlovable after all. If what she read was true, the God of the universe seemed to think she was valuable and lovely and worthwhile. Closing her eyes, Laura began to talk to Jesus about all the feelings she had hidden from everyone else for so long. Though she didn't hear an audible response, she knew without a doubt that He was listening and answering her because He loved her enough to think that what she had to say was pretty important.

TRUTH LINK:

Dear Lord, I feel like I'm at the end of myself. I'm so scared and miserable that I'm desperate to stop the pain any way I can. Please help me. Amen.

POWER UP:

God created you with purpose. He has goals, dreams, and plans that only you can fulfill. He loves you and He wants to help you. Ask Him to direct you to someone who can help you—a family member, a friend, a pastor, or someone else. Don't let yourself entertain thoughts of ending your life. You are more valuable and precious than words can ever describe, and God has a beautiful plan for your life that is more real than the hopelessness you feel right now.

COMMON GROUND

Friendship

DOWNLOAD:

Summing up: Be agreeable, be sympathetic, be loving, be compassionate, be humble. 1 Peter 3:8 THE MESSAGE

Julia looked around as she took her seat in the American history class on the first day of the school year. *Who do I know in here?* She saw a few familiar faces, but neither of her best friends. She had hoped that Lydia or Meg would be in this class, but it didn't appear that they would be. *Oh, well,* she thought.

Pulling out her notebook and pen, she noticed a new girl seated to her left. Her clothes were different than everyone else's. Not that they weren't nice, just much more monochromatic and plain. She looked different.

At the beginning of class Mr. Herr began to take roll. When he got to the new girl's name, he stumbled over it. "Laurence DuBois."

"Present," the new girl said with a lilt.

Janice, the girl seated behind her, asked, "Your name is Laurence? Isn't that a guy's name?"

"Not in my country. I am from France," she answered. Though her English was good, her accent was very thick.

Well, that explains it, Julia thought. *She's an exchange student from France. No wonder she looks different.*

Mr. Herr began to discuss what to expect throughout the year—topics, tests, papers, and projects. "Your first assignment this year is to choose an American leader and write a five-page paper on him or her. It can be a president, civic leader, or someone who has influenced the world through his or her leadership. I'll need the name of the person you will be writing about by Friday."

Around the room, whispers erupted. Everyone began to talk about who would be the topic of his or her paper. "Hey, Julia," Janice called in a hushed voice, "who are you gonna write about?"

Julia shrugged. "I don't know yet. I'll have to think about it. I'd like to write about a woman. So maybe Harriet Tubman or Amelia Earhart or Sandra Day O'Connor." As she spoke, she noticed Laurence listening.

After class Julia rose and began collecting her items. "Pardon." Julia heard the distinctive French accent directed her way. Turning around, she found Laurence smiling shyly at her. "Could you help me, please? I heard you talking about American leaders. You mentioned many. Could you make me suggestions for who to write about?"

Julia listened with a blank expression on her face. "Um, sure, I guess I could give you a few suggestions," she said. "I'll write some names down and have it to you tomorrow." Laurence thanked her and left to go to her next class.

At lunch Julia found her closest friends, Lydia and Meg. The three of them had been inseparable since elementary school. With most friendships, three's a crowd, but not with Lydia and Meg. Julia couldn't imagine two better friends. As they talked about their day, Julia felt someone standing close to her. Looking up, she found Laurence holding her lunch tray. "May I join you?" she asked.

"Sure." Julia and her friends made room for Laurence. Then Julia proceeded to introduce her to everyone.

"Where are you from?" Meg asked.

"From Toulouse, a city in France," Laurence answered.

"You're an exchange student, right?" Lydia asked. Then seeing Laurence's nod, she asked, "How long are you going to be here?"

"I will be here for one year," Laurence answered.

Julia listened to the exchange but didn't really join in. "How did you two meet?" Meg asked, pointing from Julia to Laurence.

"She's in my American history class," Julia answered simply.

"Yes, she was very kind to me. We must write a paper on a famous American, but I don't know many. Julia said she would help me choose a leader," Laurence said with obvious gratitude. Lydia and Meg immediately began naming famous Americans that Laurence could write about for her paper while Julia sat quietly.

Afterwards, Meg cornered her. "What's up? You were really quiet at lunch. Don't you like Laurence?"

Julia shrugged. "I don't know. She's okay, I guess. I'm just a little concerned she wants me to be her new best friend, you know? I just don't think we have anything in common."

Meg frowned at her and then started to laugh. "You always do this. You're immediately suspicious of people. Here's this new girl who happens to be from France. She's looking for friends, and you automatically think she's going to be a nuisance. Did you ever think you might have a lot in common with her if you just give her the chance?

Julia shrugged again and shook her head. "Fine. I'll be nice to her. I just don't want to be her one-woman cheering squad for the entire year."

Meg continued to laugh and shook her head as if to say, *Will she ever change?*

Julia knew that she was cautious when making friends, but she didn't really feel that she needed many friends. She had Meg and Lydia. That was enough. It wasn't that she was shy, but she just wasn't the type of person to have lots and lots of friends. Instead, she liked it simple—and Laurence definitely wasn't simple.

The next day in American history, Julia decided to follow Meg's advice and give Laurence a chance. She was sure they wouldn't have anything in common, but just to humor Meg, she'd do it. "Hey, Laurence, here are those American leaders that I promised you."

Laurence perused the list. "Are there any doctors here?" she asked. "I want to be a doctor when I am older."

TRUTH UNPLUGGED:

Look for the value in people and reach out to them in friendship.

Julia was surprised. She wanted to be a nurse or a doctor too. "Well, Clara Barton was a nurse, and she is the founder of the American Red Cross."

Laurence's eyes widened. "I will write about her," she said enthusiastically. "I love the Red Cross. Thank you, Julia, for your help."

Julia smiled. "So you want to be a doctor."

Laurence smiled, "*Mais oui.* My father is a doctor in France, and I want to be a doctor like him."

"Me too," Julia said with a nod. "Or a nurse. I haven't decided yet. But I know I want to work in health care." Then thinking a moment she said, "You know, I'm a candy striper at the hospital here. I volunteer with the patients—read to sick children and help the nurses and doctors."

Laurence's eyes widened again. "You are so fortunate. I would love to work at a hospital."

"Well, I don't get paid for it, but if you're interested, there's a meeting next week for new candy stripers." Julia offered, "You are welcome to come if it's okay with your host family." Excited at the prospect of becoming a candy striper, Laurence agreed to ask her family about attending the meeting.

Later Julia reflected on her conversation with Laurence. She realized that if she hadn't taken the time to reach out to Laurence, she never would have known that they had so much in common. Laurence wouldn't have made a friend and neither would Julia. By breaking out of her mold, she'd found a friend. Maybe Meg had been right. Maybe she was too suspicious of people. She was so content with her few close friends that she shut other people out.

Well, no more, she thought. *From now on, I'll try to be less suspicious of people and give them a chance. Who knows? Maybe having a lot of friends will be fun.*

TRUTH LINK:

Dear Lord, help me learn to reach out to people in friendship instead of assuming that I have nothing in common with them. I continually trust You to bring the right friends into my life. Amen.

POWER UP:

Have you ever looked at a person and immediately decided that you couldn't be friends? Maybe they dress differently or have a strange accent. Or maybe you've decided that you don't need any more friends. Be careful to give people a chance and look for the value in them—not just for them, but also for yourself. By reaching out to people and looking for common ground, you'll find that you have more in common with people than you first thought, and you'll discover that you can have more friends than you ever imagined.

THE DRIVING DILEMMA

Patience

You do not want to become lazy, but to imitate those who through faith and patience inherit what has been promised.

Hebrews 6:12 NIV

"Watch out!" Tina's father yelled from the passenger side of the car. "You have to look both ways before you pull out into traffic."

"Dad, I'm trying. You're making me nervous," Tina answered.

"Well, pay attention to where you're going!"

"Stop yelling at me!" Tina replied hotly.

"That's it," her father said with finality. "We're going home."

Walking into the house, Tina flopped onto a dining room chair. Her father had retreated into the living room and turned on the television. Turning to her mother who stood cutting up vegetables for dinner, Tina complained. "Mom, I can't take it. Dad freaks out every time I drive with him. He totally overreacts. If there's a car within a mile of me, he's sure I'm going to hit it."

Her mother smiled. "Honey, you have to be patient with him. Trust me; it's a big deal to try to teach your teenage daughter how to drive."

"Patient with him?" Tina asked in shock. "What about him being patient with me? How am I supposed to learn how to drive when he's yelling at me?" Then staring sadly down at the paper napkin she had shredded to bits, she asked, "Why can't you teach me?"

"Tina, I know this isn't easy. But it's important to your dad that he teaches you how to drive and takes you for your driving test. Just give him some time. As your driving improves, he'll relax more in the car. I promise; it'll work out."

Tina wasn't so sure. Rising from the table, she went upstairs to wash her hands and get ready for dinner. Why was her dad always so tense with her about driving? Sure, sometimes he got angry with her, but usually he was pretty cool. This was one of the first things that seemed to push him over the edge. He just got frustrated so quickly.

Over dinner, Tina sat quietly. She noticed that her father was pretty quiet too. Trying to compensate for the silence, Tina's mother and little sister chatted back and forth.

Her sister was noisily rambling on and on about her tennis lessons. Playing tennis was a family tradition. Tina had taken lessons when she was younger, and now it was Bethany's turn. "Tina, can you take me to the park tomorrow and help me with my serve?" Bethany asked excitedly. "I think I've almost got it, but I want you to show me one more time."

Tina shrugged. She'd been to the park for the past three week-ends showing Bethany how to serve or working with her on her backhand. It's not that Tina minded, but sometimes she felt like Bethany didn't listen when she tried to give her pointers. When Tina showed her a new move or tried to improve her technique, it took forever for Bethany to catch on. "I guess," Tina said. "I just don't want to go out there and waste my time. It shouldn't take forever for you to pick up each drill."

Bethany frowned down at her plate. "I do the best I can, ya know? It's not easy."

Tina didn't respond. She noticed her mother watching her with a curious expression on her face, but she couldn't dwell on it. She had other things on her mind. How was she going to learn how to drive and be ready to take her driver's test in three months? Turning to her father, she asked, "Dad, when can we practice driving again?"

Her father stopped eating and looked from Bethany to her mother before saying, "I don't know. Later."

"But, *Daaaad,* how am I supposed to be ready for my driving test?" Tina cried. She knew her father would probably get irritated at her, but she couldn't help it. She didn't want to be the *only* sixteen-year-old in school without her driver's license. She had plans. She wanted to drive her mother's car to school events and after-school band practice. If she didn't practice, she'd never be ready.

"Tina," her dad said in a tone that warned her to back off, "I said later."

Tina looked at him and then back at her mother before setting her fork down on the edge of her plate. "Fine," she said. "May I be excused? I'd like to go to my room."

TRUTH UNPLUGGED:

Patience is an attribute that you can develop through prayer and careful observation of others.

Up in her room, she sat on her bed and sulked. Her dad was being so unfair. She wasn't a bad driver, surely no worse than other kids her age. She just needed to practice. Why was he being so stubborn? And why was he so impatient with her whenever they did practice? If he would just relax, she reasoned, she'd learn and he wouldn't drive himself into a coronary.

Tap, tap, tap.

She heard a soft knock at her door. "Come in," she said.

Carefully, her mother slipped into the room. "How are you doing? You didn't eat much at dinner." Tina mumbled that she wasn't hungry, and her mother continued, "You know, your dad *is* going to teach you to drive. He just needs a little more time."

"Mom, we've been out twice now and we barely make it around the block. He gets so tense that he makes me tense. Now, he doesn't even want to take me. How am I supposed to learn?"

Her mother nodded. "You're right. He needs to have more patience with you. He can't expect you to be a professional driver the first few times you get behind the wheel."

"Exactly," Tina spit out.

Her mother continued nodding. "I know you're doing your best. You just need practice." Tina nodded, although she had a strange suspicion that she was being set up for something. "You just need someone to work with you and help you become better, like a coach."

All of a sudden, Tina saw where this was going. "You're comparing this to my teaching Bethany how to play tennis? Mom, it's not the same thing." Her mother didn't say anything. She just returned Tina's gaze. "Mom, it's not," Tina persisted. "I help Bethany all the time. She just doesn't get it. I have worked with her and worked with her. It's frustrating."

Again, her mother didn't answer. Instead, she just smiled and nodded with a humorous glint in her eye. Tina could feel her face turning red. She'd treated Bethany exactly the same way her dad had treated her. She'd gotten frustrated and short-tempered and made Bethany feel like a failure.

"Fine," she finally said. "I'll help Bethany with her tennis. I'll be more patient and I won't make her feel like a loser just because it takes her awhile to catch on."

Her mother continued smiling. "That would be really nice."

"And I'll try to give Dad a break about taking me driving. I'll try to remember that he's doing his best," she added.

Her mother walked over to her bed and sat down. Then with a hug, she said, "You're a pretty great kid, you know that? I'm really proud of you."

Tina smiled and hugged her back. "You're my mom. You have to say that." But Tina had to admit, it was a pretty nice thing to hear.

TRUTH LINK:

Dear Lord, help me to be patient with others so that I don't get irritated when they don't do something right or when things don't go my way. Instead, give me the endurance to handle things joyfully and honorably, as You would have me handle them. Amen.

POWER UP:

You know what it is to have someone lose patience with you, but do you find yourself getting easily frustrated with people or situations? Do you sometimes think, **I JUST DON'T HAVE THE PATIENCE TO DEAL WITH THIS?** Well, patience is something you can develop. You can become more tolerant with family, friends, strangers, and even situations, so that when things don't happen the way you expect or in the time frame you anticipate, you can have the grace to handle them. If you want more patience in your life, ask God to help you develop it. Then look for people in your life and in the Bible who have, or had, great patience. Learn from them and be aware of your emotions when you're in a tense situation. When you get the urge to become frustrated, take a deep breath and make the choice to remain calm. As you do, you will become a more patient person.

MORE BEAUTIFUL THAN YOU CAN IMAGINE

Death

DOWNLOAD:

None of this fazes us because Jesus loves us. I'm absolutely convinced that nothing—nothing living or dead, angelic or demonic, today or tomorrow, high or low, thinkable or unthinkable—absolutely nothing can get between us and God's love because of the way that Jesus our Master has embraced us.

Romans 8:37-39 THE MESSAGE

Danielle sat in Tiffany's bedroom. She had to get away from all the people around the house. She still couldn't believe her best friend was dead. She told herself that Tiffany was gone, but her heart just couldn't believe it. Any minute she expected Tiffany to bounce into the room, "What's wrong with you?" she would have said. "It's a beautiful day outside. Why waste it in here?"

That was Tiffany—adventurous, fun-loving, and happy. She made rooms brighter just by entering them, and people always felt better when she was around.

What am I going to do now? Danielle wondered.

Her family and friends tried to tell her that her feelings were normal, but it didn't *feel* normal. She was still in shock. At times she felt so angry she just wanted to hit something. Why had Tiffany and her family gone on vacation to Florida? They never went on vacation, so why this year? And why had Tiffany gone into the ocean that morning by herself? Danielle already knew the answer.

Tiffany had always been a strong swimmer, and there was nothing she loved more than swimming first thing in the morning. She'd been a lifeguard at the public pool, so there was no reason for her to doubt that she could handle swimming alone that morning. Unfortunately, she'd been wrong, horribly wrong. According to the Coast Guard, she'd gone out too far and gotten caught in a heavy current from which she couldn't break free. It dragged her out to sea, drowning her.

Her parents had realized she was missing when she hadn't shown up for breakfast later that morning, but by that time, it was too late. She was already gone.

Danielle continued to sit in Tiffany's bedroom. Looking around, she felt Tiffany there. She smelled her perfume. She saw the photos of Tiffany's family and friends—usually posing in some crazy, funny way—swimming trophies, and all the memorabilia that so many high school juniors have in their rooms. Then she saw the worn Bible that sat on Tiffany's dresser.

Walking over to it, she picked it up and held it close. Tiffany loved the Bible. She loved God—pure and simple. The previous summer, Tiffany had invited Danielle to attend church camp with her. "You'll love it!" Tiffany had promised, and she'd been right. Danielle had gone and been shocked to discover that something church-related was so much fun.

During that camp Danielle received Christ and dedicated her life to Him. If it hadn't been for Tiffany, she never would have discovered how fulfilling and rewarding life as a Christian could be. Before she become a Christian, she had very little hope in her life. She felt depressed and angry at the world. Since then, she'd felt at peace—peace with her parents, with her friends, and especially with herself. Instead of seeing what was wrong with her life—her parents' divorce, her brother's rebellion, and everything about herself—she now saw how blessed she was. God had given her two parents who loved her and a brother who was slowly coming around.

That's what Tiffany had done for her. More than anything else—more than friendship and more than laughter—she'd introduced Danielle to Jesus. It was a debt Danielle couldn't repay. But now what? Now Tiffany was gone and Danielle was left wondering how something so terrible could happen to someone so good.

"Danielle, are you okay?" Danielle turned to find Tiffany's mother standing at the doorway.

"Yes, I just needed to get away," Danielle said quietly. "I hope it's okay that I'm in here."

Tiffany's mother gave her a sad smile. "Of course. You know, I come in here and sit too. Somehow just being surrounded by her things makes me feel better." Danielle nodded. "I still can't believe it, you know? I replay that morning over and over in my mind, trying to figure out what I could have done differently. I could have forbidden her to go swimming alone, but she'd done it so many times before that I didn't even think about it." Tears welled up in her eyes. "I just miss her so much. Sometimes I don't know if I can make it through another day."

Danielle choked, letting the tears come that she'd held at bay all day. Then walking toward her best friend's mother, Danielle grasped her hand. They clung to each other and cried. After a few minutes, they pulled away, dried their eyes, and left to join the other guests.

As Danielle walked into the living room, she saw a handful of their friends from school. They huddled together in a corner, talking and crying. Danielle joined them. They told stories about

Tiffany. Some were funny; others were serious. They talked about missions trips to Mexico where Tiffany had given away all of her things to the poor people she'd met there. Then they told the story about the car wash fundraiser when Tiffany had doused the pastor's wife with the hose, thus starting an all-out water war. On and on the stories went. In each of them Tiffany's personality, love for people, and Jesus came through. Again, Danielle wondered how she would go on without her best friend.

Feeling that she needed some space, Danielle left to go home. She just wanted to be alone to think and pray. She knew it would be awhile before she came to terms with Tiffany's death. And although she didn't understand why it had happened, she knew that God was the only One who would get her through it intact.

TRUTH UNPLUGGED:

Death is not the end; it is the beginning of spending eternity with Christ.

When she arrived home, her mother met her at the door. Though her mother had attended the funeral, she'd only stayed a few minutes at Tiffany's house. Danielle knew Tiffany's death was hard on her mother too, because her mother kept hugging her and staring at her, as if to make certain she was still there.

"Honey, you got something in the mail today," her mother said slowly.

"Okay, what is it?" Danielle asked. Honestly, she could have cared less. She was tired and irritable and just wanted to be left alone.

Slowly her mother handed her a postcard. Danielle took it and looked at the picture on the front. Chills raced up her spine. It was a beautiful picture of the Florida coast—sandy white beaches and aqua-colored water. Turning it over, she immediately recognized Tiffany's handwriting. The words blurred as tears came to her eyes, and she realized it had been mailed the day before Tiffany died. It said:

Dear D-

You can't imagine how beautiful it is here. Pictures and stories just don't do it justice. You have to see it to believe it. I can't wait to see you again, but I know it'll be sooner than either of us realize.

Keep praying!
Tiffany

Holding the postcard close to her chest, Danielle wept. Though she knew she missed her friend—and always would—she took comfort in the fact that Tiffany was in a beautiful place with Jesus. Though it was hard to imagine not seeing her again in this world, Danielle knew they *would* see each other again. And when they did, what stories they would have to tell!

TRUTH LINK:

Dear Lord, help me to keep my eyes on You—even in the midst of losing someone. Remind me that this world is not the end, but only the beginning of spending eternity with You. Give me the strength to face my loss without getting overwhelmed by despair. You know how much I miss this person. I know it's important for me to keep living, so please help me to do that. Amen.

POWER UP:

Have you recently lost someone you love—a grandparent, a parent, a friend? It's a difficult thing to face. You may feel deep sorrow, shock, or anger. Remember that death is not the end. Be careful not to let your pain turn into hopelessness. If your loved one knew Jesus as their Savior, then they are in heaven with Him. And better yet, you'll see them again. Don't get impatient and want to go to be with them. Instead, live your life the way Jesus wants you to live it, following Him every day. As you do, He'll give you the peace, comfort, strength, and wisdom to face each day and fulfill the plans He has for you.

WHAT ABOUT THEM?

Racism

DOWNLOAD:

"Let me give you a new command: Love one another. In the same way I loved you, you love one another. This is how everyone will recognize that you are my disciples—when they see the love you have for each other." John 13:34-35 THE MESSAGE

Tammy walked into work at the DooWop Diner at 4:45 P.M. for the evening shift. It was going to be a long night. She had stayed up to finish a project for Spanish class the night before so she had gotten only a few hours of sleep. After going to school all day, here she was—ready to put in five solid hours on her feet.

She really liked her job at the diner. Harry, her boss, was nice and the atmosphere was fun. The other waiters and waitresses made it lively and action-packed between the constant jokes and the corny birthday song they had to sing whenever a customer had a birthday. It all kept her laughing, that was for sure.

As Tammy strapped on her apron, she noticed a new girl standing with Harry. The girl was obviously getting an orientation.

The thing that Tammy noticed right away was that the girl was Middle Eastern. She had an Arab face, like the ones Tammy had seen all over the news since 9/11.

Tammy hadn't ever known a Middle Easterner, but since 9/11, it didn't matter. She didn't trust any of them.

Grabbing her pen and her order pad, she walked to the front to relieve the other waitress. As she walked by Harry and the girl, he called her over. "Tammy, this is Salima. Tonight is her first night."

Tammy eyed her suspiciously and gave her a consolatory smile. "Hi," she said simply. The girl smiled back with a warm and slightly nervous smile.

"Tammy has been here for six months," Harry said. "She's a good one to ask about the way things are done around here." Tammy smiled at Harry. Then with a parting glance toward Salima, she walked away. She wasn't excited about being Salima's "go to" person. She'd prefer that Harry ask someone else, but she guessed she didn't have much choice now.

The night passed uneventfully. Tammy only talked to Salima when it was absolutely necessary. She answered her questions and showed her where things were located in the diner. She helped her with procedures and introduced her to a few of the wait staff that she hadn't met yet. Their conversations were short and to the point.

Tammy just didn't trust her.

Later that week, when a Middle Eastern family walked into the diner, Tammy hesitated. They looked like any normal family, but with past events Tammy wasn't sure she could trust them. Rather than spending the whole night feeling uncomfortable, she chose to ignore them. Before long, Salima sat them in her area.

They'll probably be more comfortable with Salima anyway, Tammy told herself. But then she thought, *I hope more of them don't start showing up.*

A few days later Tammy walked into the kitchen and noticed Salima standing in the back sniffing, like she'd been crying.

Though Tammy didn't want to get involved, her compassion won out. "Are you okay?" she asked.

Salima jerked when she heard Tammy's voice and quickly dried her eyes. "Yeah, sure. I'm fine." She straightened her apron. "I just had a rude customer."

Tammy nodded. "That happens sometimes," she said sympathetically.

"Yeah, well, these people said they refused to be waited on by an Iraqi," she said in disgust. "It's so stupid. I'm not even of Iraqi descent. And I was born in the U.S. just like they were."

Tammy didn't respond; instead, she just stood listening.

"You know, my parents came to this country to live free, just like everyone else. They just got here a little late." Salima began picking up steam as she continued. "I can't help it if I look like those crazy people from 9/11."

Tammy began to feel uncomfortable. She had to admit that she had thought the same thing as the people who had refused to allow Salima to wait on them. "You know, I kinda judged you because of the way you look too," Tammy admitted quietly.

Salima looked up and smiled through her teary eyes. "I know. I could feel it. I never used to experience much prejudice before 9/11. I mean, sure, it happened every once in a while, but in general people were nice to me and my family. Then all that changed. Now, people who

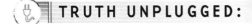

TRUTH UNPLUGGED:

Racism holds you back from experiencing the value God placed in people.

are normally really nice people look at us like we're a bunch of terrorists." Then laughing through her tears, she added, "I was actually surprised that Harry hired me. The only thing I can figure is that he's sympathetic because he's African-American."

Tammy smiled. "He's a really fair man, even more so than I am, I guess."

"Don't beat yourself up," Salima said. "It was a little weird for me after 9/11 too, just wondering who to trust. Those people were just crazy, I guess."

"Were they typical of people who practice the Islamic religion?" Tammy asked.

Salima shrugged. "I don't know. I'm a Christian. That's another reason my parents left their country. Christians were being persecuted for their religious beliefs."

"I'm so sorry," Tammy said, shaking her head. "I totally misjudged you. Here I thought you were from the Middle East and that you were Islamic and possibly a terrorist. Now I find out that you're as American as I am. We're both Christians and neither of us understand why those people did what they did on 9/11."

After accepting Tammy's apology, the two of them went back to work. As Tammy got to know Salima, she discovered that they had a lot in common. They both felt strongly about their faith. They both loved working at the diner, and they were both in the same grade in school. She also discovered that Salima had the funniest sense of humor. In time, they became great friends.

In the future, when Tammy met a person of Middle Eastern descent, she thought of Salima. Instead of letting fear and suspicion cloud her judgment, she tried to get to know the person for who they were on the inside. And though the media constantly reminded her that any Middle Easterner may be a terrorist in hiding, she lived her life the best way she could and trusted God with the rest.

TRUTH LINK:

Dear Lord, I want to love people the way You do—unconditionally, regardless of race. I pray that You'll take any racist thoughts out of my heart and mind so that I can be free to be an example of Christ in everything I do. Amen.

POWER UP:

Have you ever found yourself judging someone based on the color of their skin or ethnic origin? Maybe you've heard that a particular group of people is lazy or stingy. Maybe you've heard that they could be dangerous or take advantage of you, and because of that, you view them with suspicion or automatically dislike them. Well, watch out, you've just crossed over into racism. Racism isn't always as blatant as burning crosses in someone's front yard or using flagrant, hateful speech. It's also about automatically viewing someone with suspicion and reserve just because they're different. If you have those feelings and fears, take them to God. He wants to help free you to love people and view people the way He does. He wants and needs you to be an example of how to treat people. Remember, you are His hands and His feet in this world.

A WORLD OF DIFFERENCE

Salvation

DOWNLOAD:

Say the welcoming word to God—"Jesus is my Master"—embracing, body and soul, God's work of doing in us what he did in raising Jesus from the dead. That's it. You're not "doing" anything; you're simply calling out to God, trusting him to do it for you. That's salvation. With your whole being you embrace God setting things right, and then you say it, right out loud: "God has set everything right between him and me!" Scripture reassures us, "No one who trusts God like this—heart and soul—will ever regret it." Romans 10:9-11 The Message

Allison woke up feeling as sluggish as she had every other day. She fought to open her eyes when her alarm clock screamed at her. Rolling out of bed, she stumbled to the bathroom. Looking in the mirror, she thought, *What's the use?* She haphazardly combed her hair, brushed her teeth, and splashed water on her face. It was the least she could do without her mother having a fit.

"If you'd just try a little, you could be a very pretty girl," her mother had often said. The problem was that Allison didn't want to try. Trying required too much effort and she just couldn't be bothered.

Back in her room, she opened her closet to pull out her clothes. It wasn't as if she really had to try to find clothes that matched. Everything she had was either black or gray. Occasionally, she mixed in a white T-shirt that had splashes of red or orange on it, but that was it. She knew other girls in school dressed in the latest clothes, but Allison couldn't bring herself to do it. She hated flowers and wouldn't be caught dead in something trendy. No, she preferred jeans and T-shirts, and if she could find them both in black, so much the better.

Down in the kitchen, she poured herself a bowl of cereal and munched quietly away. "What's your day going to be like?" her mother asked cheerfully.

Allison hated these conversations; she had nothing to add. "I don't know. School, I guess," she said with a shrug. It wasn't that she was trying to be difficult or sullen; she just didn't know what else to say. Life was life, and hers was what it was.

"Honestly Allison, you make it sound as though you have it so tough," her mother said with irritation. "You know, you have it pretty good." Allison knew that without much provocation she and her mother could be in a huge fight in a matter of seconds, so she didn't answer and continued eating her cereal.

Her mother and she used to be close, but since her parents' divorce they'd drifted apart. Allison didn't really feel sad about the divorce. Sometimes she felt angry, but mostly she didn't feel anything. She knew her parents had been unhappy for years, but she'd always hoped they'd work things out. Then one day they'd made the announcement that they were separating. Six months later, their divorce became final, and six months after that, her dad had taken a job out of state. Now, she saw him on select holidays and during the summer.

Allison supposed things had been okay since then. Her mother worked long hours so they really didn't see each other much. The only time they had together was in the mornings over breakfast, and unfortunately for both of them, Allison wasn't a morning person. She didn't like to talk before 10:00 A.M. So they were left communicating through grunts in the morning and notes on the table at night.

At school, Allison drifted from class to class. She just couldn't get excited about school. She used to be an A-B student, but that was back in the days when she cared about school. Now, she found the classes boring and the other students obnoxious. She made decent grades when she tried, but without trying she could skate by with a solid C. That was good enough for her.

Lunchtime at her school had its own life. While the other students broke up into groups and noisily chatted away the hour, Allison usually bought a sandwich and drifted out to the portable classrooms to sit on the steps. Sometimes someone stopped to say hello, but most of the time she ate alone. She really didn't want to be around people; she just wanted to be left alone.

"Hey, Allison," Jenny Lipton called. Jenny was a girl in Allison's art class. She always wore T-shirts that said things like "Jesus Rocks" or "Heaven Bound."

Whatever floats your boat, Allison thought.

"I was wondering if you'd like to come to a party with me," Jenny asked.

Allison almost turned around to see if Jenny was talking to someone behind her. *Surely, she can't be talking to me.* "What kind of party?" she asked hesitantly.

"It's at a friend's house. We're going to play games and eat pizza. It'll be fun."

"Okay," Allison said before she could stop herself. After Jenny had given her all the specifics—date, time, place—and left, Allison wanted to slap herself. *Why did I say I'd go?* She had no idea.

On the night of the party, Allison arrived a few minutes late. She would have called to cancel, but realized that she didn't have Jenny's phone number. *I guess I don't have a choice,* she thought.

At the party, she looked around and realized that she didn't know any of the people there. Some looked vaguely familiar, but most were complete strangers. Allison stood on the fringe waiting for enough time to pass so that she could leave without being rude.

"Allison, come join us," Jenny called from a group playing Ping-Pong. "I'm so glad you could make it." Watching her reaction, Allison realized that Jenny really was glad to see her even though for the life of her she couldn't understand why. Most people didn't even notice Allison. She'd worked so hard to disappear that she was surprised when someone actually saw her.

After playing games for a while, everyone congregated in the living room. Allison had realized after she arrived that this was Jenny's church group. "Okay, listen up, everyone," a guy who was probably in his late twenties called, "let's bless the pizza so we can dig in."

"Dear Lord, we're here tonight to have a great time and enjoy each other's company. I pray that you would bless this food and let us have fun. I also pray that you would help any new people have a good time and feel comfortable. In Jesus' name we pray. Amen," he said and everyone gave him a hearty "Amen" in response.

After dinner, people continued to talk. Allison sat on the floor in the living room watching everyone like they were characters on a television show. They seemed to be really nice to each other in a brother-sister kind of way.

"Are you having fun, Allison?" Jenny asked as she sat down next to her on the floor.

"Yeah, it's a fun group," Allison responded. After a few seconds of silence she asked, "Jenny, why did you invite me?"

Jenny smiled at her. "I don't know. I was praying and I asked God who I should invite and your face came to my mind. I kind of took it as a sign."

Allison didn't know how to respond so she sat quietly for a few more seconds. "So do you pray often?" she finally asked.

"Yeah, I do. I talk to God about my day and what I'm thinking about and what I'm worried about and how I'm feeling about things. Stuff like that."

"And you think He hears you?" Allison asked, puzzled.

Jenny laughed. "Well, you're here, aren't you? I mean, if I hadn't prayed, then God wouldn't have made me think of you and you wouldn't have accepted. So, yeah, I think He hears me."

"That must be nice," Allison said looking away. "I mean, it must be nice to have someone who listens to you whenever you have something to say."

"You know, you can talk to Him too," Jenny said.

Allison smiled and nodded as if she knew that, but inside she wondered if God really would listen to her. Would He hear her prayers? Could she tell Him everything that went through her mind and everything she felt?

Later that night, Allison lay in bed thinking about what Jenny had said. In desperation, she closed her eyes and whispered, "God, I don't know if You can hear me or even if You care, but I'd really like to know if You're there. I don't like my life the way it is, but I don't know how to change it. Can You help?" She waited to hear an answer. When she didn't, she rolled over and closed her eyes. *Oh well,* she thought, *it was worth a shot.*

During lunch the following Monday, Allison took her regular spot on the portable steps to eat her sandwich. A few minutes after she arrived, Jenny joined her. "Hey, Allison."

"Oh hi, Jenny. Thanks again for inviting me to your party," she said.

"No problem. I'm glad you came," Jenny answered. Then shifting uncomfortably from foot to foot, Jenny said, "Listen, Allison, I was praying this weekend and I kept seeing your face in my mind. I felt like God wanted me to tell you something." Allison silently watched her. "I felt like He wanted you to know that He loves you and He sees you. And He knows you're not happy with your life the way it is and He wants to help." Allison felt the blood drain from her face. Jenny had answered the exact questions Allison had prayed.

Jenny quickly sat down beside her, "Are you okay?" Allison explained that she had prayed to God about the exact things Jenny had just said. Jenny laughed and clasped her hands together. "That's awesome!" she exclaimed.

TRUTH UNPLUGGED:

You will find no greater purpose, meaning, or fulfillment in life than that which you find in Jesus.

"What do I do now?" Allison asked in desperation.

Jenny smiled. "You can pray and ask Jesus into your heart." When Allison looked at her in confusion, she said, "Just repeat what I pray:

"Dear Lord, I know that I need You in my life, and not only do I need You, but I want You in my life. I pray that You will forgive me for my sins. I acknowledge that Jesus is the Son of God, and I dedicate my life to serving You. Please show me what to do now. Amen."

Allison repeated the prayer as Jenny said it. When she finished, she opened her eyes. She didn't know what to expect. Would there be lightning bolts? Would she now hear a voice like thunder? Instead, she felt Jenny's arms wrap around her neck. "This is so cool!" Jenny squealed.

As the weeks went by, Allison felt as though the dark cloud she had lived under had lifted. Things didn't change immediately, but as she continued to pray and read the Bible, she began to feel more hopeful about life. She went to church with Jenny, and eventually her mother joined her. *Maybe her dad would come someday too,* she thought.

She met new friends from the youth group and began to see a much bigger plan for her life. While only weeks prior she'd found it impossible to see beauty in anything, now she saw beauty everywhere. She had allowed God's unmistakable presence to come into her life, and He showed her a different world—His world filled with life.

TRUTH LINK:

Dear Lord, I believe that Jesus is the Son of God and that He died on the cross for me. I ask for Your forgiveness for my sins. I want to dedicate my life to serving You. Please help me to live the Christian life and to find Christian friends. Thank You for coming into my life. Amen.

POWER UP:

As you've read the devotions in this book, have you realized that something is missing in your life? Have you tried to find meaning in other ways, only to continue to feel a void in your life? Every single person in the world is meant to have a relationship with Jesus. Each of us decides whether to allow Him in our lives or not, but if you do, you'll find more meaning and fulfillment in life—pure and simple. He is always there waiting to listen to you, help you, and direct you. There is no greater journey you will ever take than the one you take with Jesus. Don't wait—He wants to be a part of your life today. And if you've given your life to Jesus in the past but fallen away from Him, it's okay. He still loves you. In fact, He never stopped. No matter what you've done, you're never beyond His love. Make the decision to rededicate your life to Him. Then find a church or a Christian club at school where you can make solid, Christian friends. Get ready—you've just begun the adventure of your life! And that's the Truth . . . unplugged.

TOPICAL INDEX

Anger 19

Attitude 172

Church.....................123

Cliques 71

Courage 55

Criticism..................207

Dating 9

Death 238

Difficult Parents 161

Diligence 66

Divorce 14

Drinking 49

Drugs 37

Eating Disorders 60

Encouragement 156

Family Changes 31

Fear 177

Forgiveness..............108

Friendship 228

Giving 145

Gossip.....................43

Heartbreak 166

Illness.....................202

Image 192

Inner Healing from Abuse ..133

Jealousy...................128

Joy.........................77

Judging Others...........118

Loneliness 137

Love 113

Lying......................186

Manipulation 181

Materialism................87

Mentoring 92

Modesty...................217

Patience 233

Peace 102

Persecution 151

Pornography 141

Prayer.....................141

Pregnancy 25

Pride 82

Racism....................243

Salvation 248

Sex........................118

Sibling Rivalry 197

Stealing 97

Suicide 223

Thankfulness.............212

Additional copies of this
and other Honor Books products
are available from your local bookstore.

Additional titles in this series:

Truth Unplugged–
Stories for Guys on Faith, Love, and Things That Matter Most

If you have enjoyed this book,
or if it has had an impact on your life,
we would like to hear from you.

❊ ❊ ❊

Please contact us at:

Honor Books, Dept. 201
4050 Lee Vance View
Colorado Springs, CO 80918
Or visit our website: www.cookministries.com

HONOR HB BOOKS

Inspiration and Motivation for the Season of Life